A Poetics of Orthodoxy

A Poetics of Orthodoxy

Christian Truth as Aesthetic Foundation

Benjamin P. Myers

CASCADE *Books* • Eugene, Oregon

A POETICS OF ORTHODOXY
Christian Truth as Aesthetic Foundation

Copyright © 2020 Benjamin P. Myers. All rights reserved. Except for brief quotations in critical publications or reviews, no part of this book may be reproduced in any manner without prior written permission from the publisher. Write: Permissions, Wipf and Stock Publishers, 199 W. 8th Ave., Suite 3, Eugene, OR 97401.

Cascade Books
An Imprint of Wipf and Stock Publishers
199 W. 8th Ave., Suite 3
Eugene, OR 97401

www.wipfandstock.com

PAPERBACK ISBN: 978-1-5326-9546-9
HARDCOVER ISBN: 978-1-5326-9547-6
EBOOK ISBN: 978-1-5326-9548-3

Cataloguing-in-Publication data:

Names: Myers, Benjamin P., author.

Title: A poetics of orthodoxy : Christian truth as aesthetic foundation / Benjamin P. Myers.

Description: Eugene, OR: Cascade Books, 2020 | Includes bibliographical references and indexes.

Identifiers: ISBN 978-1-5326-9546-9 (paperback) | ISBN 978-1-5326-9547-6 (hardcover) | ISBN 978-1-5326-9548-3 (ebook)

Subjects: LCSH: Poetry—History and Criticism. | Poetry—Authorship. | Spiritual life—Christianity.

Classification: PN1031 .M90 2020 (print) | PN1031 (ebook)

Manufactured in the U.S.A. DECEMBER 9, 2020

Reprinted by permission of Farrar, Straus and Giroux:
Excerpt from "Lift Off" from ALL THE WHISKEY IN HEAVEN by Charles Bernstein. Copyright © 2010 by Charles Bernstein. Excerpts from Dream Song #1 "Huff Henry" and Dream Song #80 "*Op. posth. no. 3*" from THE DREAM SONGS by John Berryman. Copyright © 1969 by John Berryman. Copyright renewed 1997 by Kate Donahue Berryman. Excerpt from "Five Houses Down" from EVERY RIVEN THING by Christian Wiman. Copyright © 2010 by Christian Wiman.

Jeanne Murray Walker, "A Gesture Upwards" from *New Tracks, Night Falling* © 2009. Wm. B. Eerdmans Publishing Company, Grand Rapids, MI. Reprinted by permission of the publisher; all rights reserved.

"Baptism" from WALKING TO MARTHA'S VINEYARD by Franz Wright, copyright © 2003 by Franz Wright. Used by permission of Alfred A. Knopf, an imprint of the Knopf Doubleday Publishing Group, a division of Penguin Random House LLC. All rights reserved.

"Farm III," copyright © 1975 by John Ashbery; from SELF-PORTRAIT IN A CONVEX MIRROR by John Ashbery. Used by permission of Viking Books, an imprint of Penguin Publishing Group, a division of Penguin Random House LLC. All rights reserved.

For my students, with whom I've discussed every idea in this book time and again over the years, and especially for Parker Hunt, whose plights and gripes are as bad as Achilles's.

Perhaps it is not too grandiose a conception to suggest that works of literature, from the short lyric to the long epic, are the recurrent discovery of the human communion *as experience*, in a definite place and at a definite time.

ALLEN TATE,
THE MAN OF LETTERS IN THE MODERN WORLD

Table of Contents

Acknowledgments xi

Introduction 1
Chapter 1: Image 17
Chapter 2: Diction 26
Chapter 3: The Sentimentality Trap 38
Chapter 4: Writing the Fallen World 52
Chapter 5: The Gift of Beauty 61
Chapter 6: Form 75
Chapter 7: Metaphor 90
Chapter 8: Mystery, Befuddlement, and Hospitality 107
Conclusion 117

Bibliography 121
Subject Index 125
Scripture Index 128

Acknowledgments

Chapter one began as a keynote address at the 2017 Forefront Conference and Festival in Rochester, New York.

Chapter two was first presented as a craft talk at the Vermont Conference on Christianity and the Arts.

Chapter three began as an address to students and faculty at Dallas Baptist University. A later version was published as "The Sentimentality Trap" in the November, 2016 issue of *First Things*. The version published here has been altered and revised.

Chapter seven originated as a paper given at the 2018 Southwest Conference on Christianity and Literature at Oklahoma Baptist University.

A small portion of chapter eight appeared as part of a review of Jae Newman's *Collage of Seoul* on the *Ruminate* blog in November of 2017.

Introduction

Art and the Church

I AM A POET and a Christian. On a few occasions I have been asked to read poems as part of a church service. This request comes from a very good impulse, and I am, of course, honored by it and happy to oblige. To be honest, however, reading poetry during a church service has usually not gone well, at least not in my experience. The congregation seems uncertain about how to react: should they applaud? Should they snap like beatniks in a coffee shop? The poems usually seem jammed into the liturgical flow rather than seamlessly integrated, interrupting worship rather than augmenting it. It is just awkward. The same thing could be said for attempts at bringing in drama, modern dance, or other art forms. It is hard not to conclude that our contemporary forms of art simply do not integrate well into the ancient rhythms of the worship service.

And yet, I maintain that the church needs art. Beyond the well-established practices of singing and instrumental music, however, we don't need the arts shoehorned into our few hours of worship on Sunday morning. Rather, we need the arts integrated into the life of the church beyond the order of worship. Christians need not just a dose of the arts but rather a whole diet of them.

We need the arts in the lives of our congregation members. The Christian life is enriched by the arts. As I try to show throughout this book, poetry can function as an antidote to the Gnosticism and disenchantment that creep into the Christian life in the contemporary world. I believe that good poetry is inherently unsecular. I trust that the same could be said of the other arts as well. In an age of overwhelming superficiality, when an endless driveling stream of mindless entertainment is always just a click away, the arts help to nudge the Christian toward a richer, ancient path and anchor the Christian into the life more abundant to which our savior calls us. The arts call us to take creation seriously, to honor God as *the* Creator. Since God is the origin of all that is beautiful, since God is indeed beauty itself, I do not see how any way of life indifferent to beauty could be considered an authentic Christian life.

We should thus make the arts as much a part of Christian family life as devotional times and *Veggie Tales*. We should teach our children to love the Lord our God, who is the God not only of moral uprightness but also of beauty and of meaning: the God of righteousness *and* glory. This means sharing the expressly Christian arts with our children, by, for instance, reading them stories by L'Engle, Lewis, and Tolkien, memorizing together poems by George Herbert and Gerard Manley Hopkins, listening to the music of Bach, and looking at the paintings of Rembrandt.

It also means sharing even the non-Christian arts together, as a clear example of God's "common grace." Art is something that God has given to all the creatures made in his image. God is so good that he allows even his rebellious creatures—looking at artists in the modern world, some might say some of his *most* rebellious creatures—to echo his creative goodness through creations exhibiting great beauty and containing great depth. What, then, if our families were in the habit of sharing art of all kinds together as a family, the way we share a meal? And what if we were in the habit of "saying grace" over the bountiful gift of creativity in the same way we do over the gift of nourishment through food? What, then, might our children learn about the endless depth of God?

And what if we were in the habit of bringing the arts into the church building? Again, because God is the source of all beauty, is ultimate Beauty itself, we should care as much about the quality of art on the walls of our churches and Sunday school rooms as we do about the "message." We should not allow a reductive rationalism of modernity to convince us that God is proclaimed only through sermons. In fact, we should care about how the very walls of the church look, renewing our sense of a truly, deeply Christian architecture as alien to the utilitarian modes of modernism or the merely disposable forms of much contemporary architecture. Moreover, we should be willing to study poetry, painting, and more in our Sunday school classes and in our discipleship courses, looking to great Christian art for

Introduction

inspiration and guidance and looking to the art of secular modernity to foster our understanding of and compassion for those lost in the world around us.

We need the arts also in our Christian universities, as an antidote to the materialism and utilitarianism of our times and, sadly, of our educational cultures. The arts help our students to see that there is more to life than a good salary and well-financed leisure time. The arts expand a student's concept of what it means to be a human being made in the image of God. A good foundation in the arts during the university years may not especially prepare a student for his or her work, but it just might give a student the spiritual and emotional wherewithal to make it through a period of unemployment. It will certainly dignify and enrich the leisure hours and magnify the resources that a student brings to meditating on God's word.

But, in order for the arts to enrich the life of the church, we need both an openness to amateur attempts and a critical sense of what makes for excellence in the arts. We need a church culture in which everyone is encouraged to express himself or herself creatively but in which only the most seriously pursued and thoughtfully realized of these expressions is presented to the whole congregation and to the wider world. We need a culture of arts in the church that allows all of God's children to explore the artistic impulse but that also maintains space for thinking about "whatever is lovely, whatever is commendable" and where "there is any excellence" and "anything worthy of praise" (Philippians 4:8). That would be a culture that values the gift of creativity in all people but also values unique individual gifts and the gift that is real beauty itself. To commend we must have a sense of what is commendable. We need a church that takes creativity seriously enough to see that everybody has it, but not everybody has it in the same way or to the same extent in all possible areas of expression, a church that encourages hobby art yet uniquely celebrates art of special accomplishment.

Despite the fact that throughout this book I will put forth a scheme of thought by which to make critical judgements about the art of poetry, I want to emphasize that we should be very careful about rushing to criticism when an artist is beginning to practice his or her art. We need to create amateur spaces for artists, resisting the urge to rush them into public view but also resisting the urge to squash their creative impulse. We should fight the vague notion current in our culture that only professionals can make art and only academics can understand it. The fact that not all pianists can or should aim for playing Carnegie Hall should deter us neither from encouraging dalliance nor from recognizing excellence.

Before so much of our leisure was gobbled up by big screens at home and little screens in our hands, amateur involvement in the arts was far more common among adult Americans. One did not have to be an English professor to read poetry and maybe even write a little for special occasions. One did not need to be a renowned professional musician to play the piano for family gatherings or even just to pass an evening singing around the spinet. Small towns throughout the country offered community orchestras, community theater, and art fairs. Not too long ago in America, the arts were as much a part of life as sports are today.

My grandparents, born in the early twentieth century, had only minimal education, up through the eighth grade in a one-room schoolhouse in the mountains of eastern Oklahoma, yet well into their old age they loved to recite poetry by the likes of Longfellow and to make up songs and rhymes. That is to say nothing of the high art they made of storytelling. Art was a part of life. To make art was normal.

My grandparents, however, did not expect a record contract or publishing deal. They did not expect their artistic efforts to reach beyond their close circle of friends and kin. More to the point, they admired the efforts of accomplished artists far more than their own efforts and encouraged their children to pursue an education and to read. They recognized, implicitly, a legitimate hierarchy of aesthetic success. Although they wouldn't articulate it this way, this was the case because they inherited a long-standing view in the Christian world regarding the relationship between God and the three "transcendentals" of truth, goodness, and beauty. One need not study medieval philosophy to grasp that God is the highest good (Psalm 119:68), the highest truth (John 14:6–7), and the highest beauty (Psalm 27:4), and that all truth, goodness, and beauty we encounter in this world thus point us toward God. Truth, goodness, and beauty are in some sense markers of God's presence. They are transcendental signifiers of the Divine Being. The more truth, goodness, and beauty of which a thing is possessed, the more it testifies of the highest truth, goodness, and beauty.

Aesthetic standards are thus a direct result of our understanding of who God is. To live in accordance with the high Christian calling and the life more abundant promised us by Christ is, in part, to pursue truth, goodness, and beauty to the greatest extent possible. Thus we dwell on "whatever is true, whatever is honorable, whatever is just, whatever is pure, whatever is lovely, whatever is commendable" (Philippians 4:8). We do not, or at least should not, give our attention to just "whatever."

The Return of Standards

Already, I can imagine some readers objecting. They are thinking, "Can we really say that one poem is better than another? Doesn't it all depend on preferences? Isn't the evaluation of poetry, after all, simply a matter of personal taste?" We expect almost everything to depend on mere preference in our world of endless consumer choices.

Many people today, saturated as our culture is in a soft postmodernism that resists all hierarchies of value, would say that any poem a reader happens to enjoy is just as good as any other poem, that an "instapoet" posting his cliché-riddled musings on social media is as worthy of our time as Emily Dickinson. To the casual postmodernist, outside of and inside of the church, all values are subjective and relative. It just depends on what one likes. "Beauty is in the eye of the beholder."

But it is the contention of this book not only that we can discern those qualities that make a poem good (and thus make one poem better than another), but also that the criteria for making such aesthetic judgements are implicit in basic Christian orthodoxy. The most important truths of our reality—who God has revealed himself to be and what he has done in Jesus Christ to bring about the redemption of both the believer and all of creation—are the logical place to look when we seek to ground our aesthetic understanding on something firmer than the shifting sands of personal taste or cultural trends. The directive to focus our attention on "whatever is true, whatever is honorable, whatever is just, whatever is pure, whatever is lovely, whatever is commendable," is indeed a far cry from a simple "whatever" with a shrug. As Scripture clearly contradicts our cultural impulse to assume that beauty is in the eye of the beholder, the properly Christian response to art isn't to say, "It's all good as long as the artist likes it." Although criticism of someone else's artistic efforts may make us uncomfortable, we can't be content with just "being nice," because we have to take cultural stewardship more seriously than that. Solid aesthetic judgement begins with sound theology. Appreciating poetry can begin with the Apostles' Creed.

The idea that we have no basis on which to pronounce one work of art superior to another is relatively new in our culture. Its roots are in Romanticism, but it doesn't really become widespread until postmodernism begins to trickle down from university departments of English into the aesthetic judgements of the general population. In its rejection of all "metanarratives"—those overarching stories, such as Christianity, that give shape and meaning to life—postmodernism asserts that all value judgments, whether moral or aesthetic, hold true only for the individual asserting them. For the thoroughgoing postmodernist, a Spider-Man comic is as inherently worthwhile as *Hamlet*. The true postmodernist lives by the credo "Who am I to judge?"

Of course, bad taste has always been with us, but prior to our own epoch most people would either have believed their own bad taste to be good taste (not just personally but universally) or they would have, at least, been embarrassed by their preference for lesser works of art over greater. But today "lesser" and "greater" are nearly extinct terms in the evaluation of art, including poetry. Today every aesthetic judgement is preceded by an explicit or implicit prepositional phrase, "for me."

Of course, some professional critics, such as we have left, still maintain some objective criteria, usually implicit but occasionally explicit, for evaluating new poetic works. It is generally impossible, however, to find any foundation on which such criteria may rest. Most general readers, moreover, have no particular basis for their opinions about poetry or art of any kind. In fact, I suspect many general readers today avoid poetry as a category simply because they have no way of knowing which poems may be worth their time.

What's worse, many aspiring poets today—indeed, many poets already presenting their work to the public—have no sense of even a minimal aesthetic standard that they should aim to meet. The poetry world continues to speak of "excellence" and to hand out prizes and fellowships, but there is little to no sense of a shared set of aesthetic criteria.

I argue for orthodoxy not as an arbitrary standard for poetic achievement, but as a reality-based way of knowing what kinds of poetry, what poetic characteristics, most resonate with true human experience. I take orthodoxy to be not an arbitrary list of theological standards forced on the many by the few, but rather the consensus arrived at by the Christian intellectual tradition as it seeks to describe the true nature of reality. In short, I don't believe that, say, the doctrine of the Trinity is true because the church says so, but rather that the church says so because it is true. Precisely because it is not the work of a single person but rather a thoroughly worked-out consensus over time and precisely because it does not bend to accommodate itself to any one person's preference, I take Christian orthodoxy to be the best place to look for a fundamental understanding of how human beings experience the world. This ability to describe our experience of reality makes orthodoxy the logical place to begin in understanding how good art resonates with our truest, most profound perceptions of what it means to be human.

I was a writer before I was a Christian, and, after I came to Christ, I marveled at the rich resources for aesthetics found in the Christian faith. Doctrinal essentials such as the incarnation and the Trinity provide Christianity with a firm foundation on which to build a poetics, as Christianity articulates expectations about the nature of reality that can in turn shape our expectations of art.

Insisting on a poetics of orthodoxy, however, can be an invitation to misunderstanding. The issue I am concerned with is not whether or not a particular poem expresses orthodox theological sentiments, a crude form of criticism indeed that has little to do but berate John Milton's *Paradise Lost* for the possible Arian heresy of its author. Rather, I assert that what is good in poetry of any sort—as much amidst the heresies of William Blake or the unbelief of Percy Shelly as amidst the faithful praises of Gerard Manley Hopkins or in the later, post-conversion work of T. S. Eliot—is what resonates on the aesthetic plane with truth on the propositional plane of Christian orthodoxy.

I hope to show how Christian orthodoxy, the "faith that was once for all delivered to the saints" (Jude 3) can inform the taste of the poetry writing and reading public. I aim to give the Christian poet some explicit guidelines for crafting aesthetically successful poems. I also aim to give the general reader a way to evaluate poetry, to tell the good from the bad.

There is a need for aesthetic standards that make sense to the church. The modern church lacks a clear aesthetic, and the result is that the church often associates itself with tacky, low-quality art or is indifferent to the arts altogether. This is a failure of cultural stewardship. Thus literary criticism can be a form of what the contemporary artist Makoto Fujimura calls "culture care." Fujimura says, "Culture care is to provide care for our culture's 'soul,' to bring to our cultural home our bouquet of flowers so that reminders of beauty—both ephemeral and enduring—are present in even the harshest environments where survival is at stake."[1] Poetry can give us flowers only if we tend the soil and nurture the blossoms. This book offers

---

1. Fujimura, *Culture Care*, 22.

tips for the growth and care of poetry in particular, but many of the criteria it establishes for the evaluation of poems can be easily transferred to other forms of art. I imagine no art form can work independently of who we are as creatures who are embodied yet made in the image of God, sinful yet offered redemption in Christ, walking through the valley of the shadow of death yet already being made to lie down in green pastures. Good art resonates with who we are, and Christian orthodoxy has some very particular and clear things to say about who it is that we are.

While my main focus is how faith can illuminate the quality of art, this book is also about what the arts, particularly poetry, can bring to the church. Along the way, we shall see that not only does Christian orthodoxy give us criteria for good poetry but also that good poetry helps us to see the richness and depth of Christian orthodoxy. The life of art and the life of faith can not only coexist but actually reinforce one another.

My friend the naturalist, apologist, Inklings scholar, novelist, and computer scientist Matthew Dickerson, likes to use J. R. R. Tolkien's short story "Leaf by Niggle" to talk about the relationship between art and the Christian faith. In the story, we come to see that Niggle's painting, while not amounting to much in his lifetime and not remembered after his death, was pointing all the time toward the eternal. We come to see, that is, that beauty points us toward God. Along the way, however, we also get a glimpse of how the artist relates to the rest of the congregation, as we see Niggle's work frequently interrupted by his neighbor, the conspicuously named Mr. Parish. It is only when they are reunited on the other side of death that Niggle and Mr. Parish see how they always needed each other, how they are, biblically speaking, parts of the same body. It is my hope that this book will give us a glimpse of the importance of the relationship between artist and congregation while we are both still on this side of eternity.

Largely, I will proceed by means of contrast. The best way to illustrate the resonance between good poetry and good theology is to examine the contrast of both with one of the most persistent heresies in the Christian tradition: Gnosticism.

Recovering from Gnosticism

In a manner of speaking, orthodox Christians owe a lot to the gnostic heretics who infiltrated the church in its early years. It was the various doctrines of "secret knowledge" promulgated by Gnosticism that forced the first theologians of orthodoxy, such as Iranaeus, to begin the long, arduous task of outlining a systematic Christian theology. Speaking of Iraneus's *Against Heresies*, written in the late second century, church historian and theologian Harold O. J. Brown says, "It is possible to say that Gnosticism is in a sense the stepmother of systematic theology and that a heresy is the stepmother of orthodoxy."[2] Augustine himself says something similar in his *Confessions:* "The rejection of heretics brings into relief what your church holds and what sound doctrine maintains."[3] In a process surprisingly similar to modern academic science with its emphasis on experiment and peer-review, by rejecting error, the church came to better understand the truth.

The gnostic influence is perhaps stronger now than at any time since its original vanquishing by the fathers of the church. Postmodern Americans spend their lives disembodied in little screens, detached from the reality of God's creation around them, including the human creation. Facebook is obviously not a book, but neither is it a face. Postmodern people have come to believe that we can ignore the *givenness* of creation, bending physical reality to suit our inner life. So-called "transhumanists" have begun to champion our supposedly impending ability to upload what they see as our core selves—that is, whatever is *not* the body—into computer code to live forever. Contemporary folly is, to a great extent, gnostic folly, and it is penetrating even our churches.[4] As Alister McGrath points out, Gnosticism appeals to contemporary sensibilities, and "[i]ts echo is heard today in those who interpret Christianity as a religion of self-discovery, not redemption. Religion is the quest for true inner identity, the 'real me,' the inner spark of divine life, or the gold in the mud."[5] He is describing the contemporary church in its familiar guise of self-help group, our suffering and redeeming Christ reduced to a guru who will help you find your best life now.

This version of the heresy can be obvious, but it surfaces perhaps even more frequently in more subtle, pious sounding phrases. Any time we dismiss material reality in favor of an airy spirituality, any time we reduce the body God has fearfully and wonderfully made to the status of a "mere container," we step into the gnostic heresy. This is the legacy of Gnosticism: a faith detached from creation itself.

2. Brown, *Heresies,* 42.

3. Augustine, *Confessions,* 129.

4. For a thorough account of heresy in contemporary culture, in and out of the church, see Douthat, *Bad Religion.*

5. McGrath, *Heresy,* 232.

A Poetics of Orthodoxy

This contempt for the physical givenness of humanity, this disdain for creation, has long pushed at the borders of the Christian faith. Beginning, in fact, long before the time of Christ, there were those who taught that only spirit is good, that matter is by default and always low and unworthy. Plato—for all his virtues and for all that he has given orthodoxy through his distant pupil Augustine—is perhaps not the originator of but certainly a major contributor to this error, in his insistence that the physical world is mere illusion compared with the realm of ideas. But Plato, at least, saw value in this world's reflection of the ideal world, and he passed on to many of his Christian admirers that sense of creation's value as a pointer toward the transcendent. By the first century AD, however, many in the Greco-Roman culture insisted on a firm dualism in which all that is immaterial is good and all that is material is bad. Though there were many forms of gnostic thought in the ancient world, it is that which penetrated the fledgling Christian church which we call *Gnosticism*. The gnostic teachers insisted on arcane, occult knowledge—*gnosis* is Greek for knowledge—which they maintained was the path to salvation. This *gnosis* is too needlessly complex to rehearse here, but it was most likely the gnostics' complex system of *eons*—apparently the offspring of gods, angels, and abstract ideas—that prompted Paul to warn against "genealogies" in Titus (3:9).

Most simply put, Gnosticism attempted to foist two main errors onto the early Christian church: a denial of the goodness of creation and a denial of the incarnation of Jesus Christ. The gnostics rejected Genesis 1:31 in its insistence that "God saw everything that he had made, and behold, it was very good." In fact, they often insisted that God himself, or at least "the God of the Old Testament" is evil, since only an evil God could do something so vile as create the physical universe and imprison man's soul in a body. Not surprisingly, they also rejected John 1:14, which claims that "the Word became flesh and dwelt among us." They embraced instead what has come to be known as *docetism*, the belief that Jesus, as God, only *appeared* to take on human flesh.

These two errors were immediately identified by the early church as being well outside the pale of orthodoxy. Yet, one suspects it wouldn't take much digging to find similar, though only vaguely defined, errors today even in congregations that consider themselves defenders of orthodoxy. It is always tempting to fall into airy spiritualizing and disdain for the body. It is always far too easy to so love Jesus as God that we forget to love him as the God who became man.

Introduction

There are overt gnostics today, people who intentionally claim the mantle of the ancient heresy, but they are few and far between. Far more of a problem is the general Gnosticism of our culture and the subtle drifting within the church itself that we might refer to as "creeping Gnosticism." As the Canadian philosopher Charles Taylor argues in *A Secular Age,* his monumental study of secularization, "official Christianity has gone through what we can call an 'excarnation', a transfer out of embodied, 'enfleshed' forms of religious life, to those which are more 'in the head'. In this it follows in parallel with 'Enlightenment', and modern unbelieving culture in general."[6] Protestants, with our traditional iconoclasm, are prone to throw the baby (the goodness of creation) out with the bathwater of idolatry. Having rejected the extreme asceticism of some of the mystical and monastic traditions, we have replaced it with a more selfish asceticism that allows us to be as comfortable and well-fed as we wish as long as we deprive ourselves of beauty. Perhaps it is time to consider whether an ugly church building might suggest an unknowingly gnostic congregation worships inside.

At the very least, we can see in the gnostic heresy an easily discernable magnification of errors we ourselves all too easily drift into. The ancient gnostics were prone on the one hand to an extreme asceticism—a hatred for the body God had given—that induced them to a legalistic view of salvation. They reviled what God has called good and given to us. On the other hand, gnostics often stretched indifference to the body to the point that they saw sins of the flesh as insignificant. They asserted that it doesn't matter what vile things they do with their bodies as long as their souls are pure. Ancient gnostics, like many contemporary congregants, tended toward either prudishness or licentiousness, or perhaps to wild swings between the two extremes.

The early church responded to the pressures of Gnosticism, which found enthusiastic following in the Mediterranean world, with the canonization of Scripture, the endeavors of theology, and the crafting of the creeds. The Apostles' Creed is credited by tradition to the apostles themselves, and, while that origin is probably more fanciful than true, we can find versions of the creed circulating by the late second century. The version used today in churches ranging from Catholic to Presbyterian was finalized by the sixth century.[7] As translated in *The Book of Common Prayer,* it reads as follows:

6. Taylor, *A Secular Age,* 554.
7. Cannata and Reitano, *Rooted,* 6.

I believe in God the Father Almighty,
Maker of heaven and earth:

And in Jesus Christ his only Son our Lord,
Who was conceived by the Holy Ghost,
Born of the Virgin Mary,
Suffered under Pontius Pilate,
Was crucified, dead, and buried:
He descended into hell;
The third day he rose again from the dead;
He ascended into heaven,
And sitteth on the right hand of God the Father Almighty;
From thence he shall come to judge the quick and the dead.

I believe in the Holy Ghost;
The holy Catholic Church;
The Communion of Saints;
The Forgiveness of sins;
The Resurrection of the body,
And the Life everlasting.
Amen.

These words are aimed at differentiating orthodox Christianity from Gnosticism, by first emphasizing God as creator and by then enumerating events in the physical life of Christ. Notice, too, that the resurrection of the body precedes and leads into the life everlasting. Matter is not merely temporary in orthodox Christianity. Our bodies were originally made for eternity and will be restored to live in eternity. The creed insists on a God who made matter good and who entered it not to defeat it but to redeem it. According to the earliest statements of Christian belief, redemption is not a process of making matter irrelevant but rather of making it permanent.

Orthodox Christianity has always been, to borrow the term coined by Umberto Eco, "pancalistic" in its outlook.[8] Eco's invented word means something like "all-that-is-is-good-istic." That is, orthodox Christianity takes seriously God's evaluation of his own work in Genesis 1:31 and affirms the goodness of all that God has created. This vision is not a denial of the fall but rather a looking back through the results of sin to see the

---

8. Eco, *Art and Beauty*, 17.

INTRODUCTION

goodness of God's original creation. It, in fact, recognizes that the doctrines of fall and redemption make no sense without a primal goodness of creation. In his *Confessions*, Augustine argues that "things which are liable to corruption are good. If they were the supreme goods, or if they were not good at all, they could not be corrupted. For if they were supreme goods, they would be incorruptible. If there were no good in them, there would be nothing capable of being corrupted."[9] Augustine insists that even the corruptible things of this world have the goodness of their being from God. Theologians from Augustine, through Aquinas, Luther, Calvin, and down to the present have insisted that the things of this world should never be confused with the *summum bonum* (highest good) which is God, but neither should they be confused with the total lack of good we call evil. As much as he regretted his overattachment to the things of this world and as much as he owes Plato as a model for his thought, Augustine was no gnostic and no despiser of God's handiwork.

No matter how "otherworldly" it can seem in expression, the historic Christian faith has at its center the redemption of *this* world, the eventual glory of *this* body. Even Dante's *Paradiso*, which in its scholastic ponderings can seem so abstract in comparison to his *Inferno* and the *Purgatorio*, emphasizes the pancalistic nature of the faith. When Dante encounters the blessed and shining spirit of Solomon himself, inhabiting the sphere of the Sun with other philosophers and theologians, the wisest of all men tells the pilgrim that

> But even as a coal that sends forth flame,
> And by its vivid whiteness overpowers it
> So that its own appearance it maintains,
>
> Thus the effulgence that surrounds us now
> Shall be o'erpowered in aspect by the flesh,
> Which still to-day the earth doth cover up[.][10]

Even Solomon's spirit in Heaven does not shine like the body that waits beneath the earth will someday shine with the light of Holiness. This view of the body, indeed of all matter, as glorious because it is made by God is essential in the true Christian faith and has been maintained as an important element of orthodoxy since the early days of the church.

---

9. Augustine, *Confessions*, 124.
10. *Paradiso* 14.52–57 (trans. Longfellow).

A Poetics of Orthodoxy
Art Against the Gnostics

To the Gnosticism that continues to creep in today, we too can respond with Scripture, theology, and creed. But we can also respond with art. Good art, art that insists on particularity and that resists sentimentality, is the natural foe of gnostic heresy. As Charles Taylor points out, "excarnation" is importantly resisted by "aesthetic experience, where embodied feeling can still be allowed to open us to something higher."[11] The path to holiness is not to forget the earth but to reconnect it to heaven. The awe we feel in the great cathedrals isn't due simply to the heights above us. After all, we walk everyday under a limitless sky. At least part of the awe we feel in Chartres or Notre Dame is from looking up to see the stones of the earth inhabiting such heights. Similarly, good poetry is always on the side of embodiment and honesty, even when the poet himself is unware. William Blake famously—and mistakenly—claimed that John Milton, his beloved poetic precursor, was "of the Devil's party without knowing it." I believe many great poets have been of God's party, often without knowing it.

The Christian poet, however, should know it. The Christian artist should work consciously on behalf of the faith, not only through polemic and preaching, but also through the good work of creation. The poem, the painting, the sculpture, to be truly Christian, I believe, must be focused on the particular, the created. As Harold O. J. Brown says, "Christianity is distinguished from the more speculative great religions such as Hinduism and Buddhism by its absolute dependence on the *historicity* and *particularity* of the Gospel. Jesus is indeed called the *Logos* ('Word') and the Mediator between God and man, but he is not seen as a cosmic or universal principle, but as a real flesh-and-blood human being, who suffered, died, and rose again under a real, historical, and trivial Roman official, Pontius Pilate."[12] The gnostic seeks to liberate spirit from matter; the poet works in, and celebrates, the union of the two. Thus both art and faith should always be cognizant of detail, of concreteness, and of context.

In his *Confessions*, Augustine tells how noticing the particular things of creation points us toward the creator God. Were we just to admire the object, of course, we would be in danger of idolatry. But when we allow our focused attention to point us through the object at the source of all being, then we have turned attention into prayer. Augustine writes, "And I said to

---

11. Taylor, *A Secular Age*, 288.
12. Brown, *Heresies*, 45.

INTRODUCTION

all these things in my external environment: 'Tell me of my God who you are not, tell me something about him.' And with a great voice they cried out: 'He made us' (Ps. 99: 3). My question was the attention I gave to them, and their response was their beauty."[13] God speaks to us through beauty. Our attention to the particulars of the world—which is given in contemplation, in study, and in good art—honors God.

Thus, in its opposition to creeping Gnosticism, poetry reinforces the Christian concept of redemption. Romans 8:20–23 says, "For the creation was subjected to futility, not willingly, but because of him who subjected it, in hope that the creation itself will be set free from its bondage to corruption and obtain the freedom of the glory of the children of God. For we know that the whole creation has been groaning together in the pains of childbirth until now." The goodness that remains in the fallen world yearns to be redeemed. Only Jesus' work on the cross, of course, can bring about this redemption, but poetry mirrors redemption. Good poetry is a participation in redemption, a joining with Christ in his good work. Poetry can help us meet Wendell Berry's admonition to "Practice resurrection."[14]

James K. A. Smith clarifies Taylor's point about "excarnation" by saying, "In contrast to the central conviction of Christian faith—that the transcendent God became *in*carnate, en-fleshed, in Jesus of Nazareth—*ex*carnation is a move of disembodiment and abstraction, an aversion of and flight from the particularities of embodiment (and communion)."[15] I believe excarnation is damaging to our churches, our larger culture, and our art. This book is about how to achieve and recognize good poetry and about how poetry, when it is good, can help us achieve, in a sense wholly commensurate with Christian orthodoxy, a kind of "re-incarnation." I mean by that not, of course, the transmigration of souls imagined by Pythagoras or by Eastern religions, but rather a return to a way of life more fully embodied in God's good creation.

---

13. Augustine, *Confessions*, 183.

14. Berry, "Manifesto: The Mad Farmer Liberation Front," in *The Country of Marriage*, 17.

15. Smith, *How (Not) to be Secular*, 58.

I

Image

What We Learn from Imagism

IMAGE IS A LOADED word in Christian circles. The second commandment instructs us not to make any "graven images," and the very word *image* brings to mind the long conflict in Christianity between icon and iconoclasm. One thinks of the sixteenth-century Puritans whitewashing over frescoes in country churches and smashing stained glass windows in cathedrals. I belong to a denomination in that radical reformation tradition that has long been especially skeptical of religious images, and the sanctuary I worship in several times a week is devoid of anything like representational art. Yet, not only am I strongly drawn to the artistic traditions of Christendom—to Carvaggio's *The Entombment of Christ* (1602–1603) and to Eugène Burnand's *The Disciples Peter and John Running to the Sepulcher on the Morning of the Resurrection* (c. 1898), for instance—but I also can't help but think that any poem that fails to make concrete, particular imagery an integral part of the poem is an artistic failure. I don't think this is a contradiction. Our faith clearly demands we never elevate the things of this world to the status of God, and thus we are prohibited from making "images" in that sense. Yet our faith also demands we recognize both the goodness of creation and our inherent nature as embodied beings, a recognition greatly aided by the making of images in a very different, artistic, sense.

A Poetics of Orthodoxy

Certainly I'm not the first to feel that clear, definite imagery is an indispensable part of poetry. In the early twentieth century, the poetic movement known as "Imagism" sought to focus modern poetry on the task of clearly presenting a series of images—or even one image, such as in William Carlos Williams's "The Red Wheelbarrow"—with absolute clarity. Ezra Pound, the major force behind the movement, insisted that the goal of poetry ought to be "Direct treatment of the 'thing,' whether subjective or objective."[1] Perhaps the imagists were driven by a need to find a new core for defining poetry as the new free verse blurred once clear distinctions between poetry and prose. Certainly, they saw themselves as reacting against the rhetorical excesses of Victorian and Romantic poetry.

They were not, however, merely destructive modernists. Pound found inspiration for his poetics in Homer, Dante, and perhaps most of all the classical Chinese poets who had made clarity of image a chief poetic virtue. That is to say, "Imagism" was a reform movement, not a revolution. It sought to return poetry to its essential elements and took clarity of image, concreteness, to be perhaps the most essential thing in a poem. The imagists saw clearly that the focused, specific image has always been an integral part of the best poems. When Pound declaimed that the poet should "Go in fear of abstractions," he was not abolishing the poetic law but fulfilling it.[2]

Though Pound and his fellow *Imagistes* could be doctrinaire at times —Hugh Kenner described Imagism as "a technical hygiene"—they call our attention to the central role of the particular, concrete image in the making of good poetry.[3] Like the Japanese haiku masters, they remind us that particularity is at the heart of great poems.

In his justly famous "In a Station of the Metro," Pound, inspired by the Japanese haiku tradition, whittled what was originally a thirty-line poem down to create a minimalist masterpiece.[4] The powerful emotion of the poem is conveyed entirely in the concentrated images:

> The apparition of these faces in the crowd;
> Petals on a wet, black bough.[5]

---

1. Pound, *Literary Essays*, 3.
2. Pound, *Literary Essays*, 5.
3. Kenner, *The Pound Era*, 178.
4. Kenner, *The Pound Era*, 184.
5. Pound, "In a Station of the Metro," in *Selected Poems*, 35.

The emotion of the poem is inherent in our visualization of the blossoms of a flowering tree in wet weather: at no point are we directly *told* how to feel. Yet the emotional tone, the *pathos,* of the poem is unmistakable. Pound says that "An 'Image' is that which presents an intellectual and emotional complex in an instant of time."[6] In this great poem, the emotion is nuanced, complex, unparaphraseable, yet apparent.

Consider how much less effective, and affecting, "In a Station of the Metro" would be if Pound had written something like this, instead:

> I'm all alone in the crowd.
> The people move by so separate from me,
> So distant and so beautiful.
> I feel alone,
> I feel so alone.
> Why can't I reach their beautiful inner selves?
> Why do I ache with pain
> And with joy?

Not only is the bad version more than twice as long as Pound's poem, but also it says not even half as much. I doubt the poem above has the ability to make anyone actually sad. It attempts only to "convey" how the author feels. The original version, rather, conveys the reader into the experience of the poet. One can't affect the reader's emotions through direct emotional instructions like "feel sad." One has to conjure sadness as it is experienced by embodied human beings. This is why "show; don't tell" is classic advice in all forms of writing.

The Word Became Flesh

Why does the pale imitation of Pound's poem, an imitation wholly and overtly concerned with an emotion that is only implied in Pound's minimalist masterpiece, carry so much less emotional power than Pound's poem, which says nothing directly about the feelings of the poet? The answer lies in the orthodox Christian assertion that we are all embodied beings.

Unlike Gnosticism, orthodox Christianity does not consider the human creation to be fundamentally a soul trapped in a body but rather a being made of body and soul. Christians do, of course, affirm a distinction

---

6. Pound, *Literary Essays,* 4.

between the body and the soul, but a biblical anthropology that keeps both the Genesis account of our creation and the promised resurrection in mind rejects the pop-culture Gnosticism that says we are *really* souls confined in a body we will someday be free from. Our bodies are in a real sense *us,* not just the containers in which we are held until we can be released for heaven. The separation of body and soul that we call death is not our end goal but only a temporary stage, for those who die before the great day, before the eternal resurrected life. Christians, of all people, should be most willing to understand our experience of the world in physical terms, without limiting that experience to the material. We are body *and* soul.

We thus have no experiences of emotion outside of our body. If you have loved, then you have loved at a particular time, in a particular place, with a particular physical sensation present in your bodily self. You have been hungry while in love. You have been seasick while in love. You have been in love under the shade of a great oak tree or in the glaring sun. You have never been in love nowhere and without your body. When a man remembers his wedding, he remembers standing at the altar, his bride walking down the aisle toward him, perhaps the pendant lights of the church or the little birds moving about in the bushes around the gazebo. He does not, I'd wager, primarily remember a legal change of status. "Love" may be an abstract noun, but love is among the least abstract of all human experiences.

Despite the gnostic trends of much of the contemporary church, our experience of God is also largely both spiritual and physical. The liturgy of the church has traditionally reminded us of this, as we stand, sit, and kneel. Even closer to the subject of poetry, we should think also about the physicality of the Psalms. The first psalm doesn't just tell us that goodness is healthy; it tells us that the righteous man "is like a tree / planted by streams of water." Psalm 18 doesn't merely mention that God is victorious over his enemies; it puts us there to see them destroyed:

> And he sent out his arrows and scattered them;
> he flashed forth lightnings and routed them.
> Then the channels of the sea were seen,
> and the foundations of the world were laid bare
> at your rebuke, O Lord,
> at the blast of the breath of your nostrils. (Psalm 18:14–15)

God's nostrils! Of course, God the Father doesn't actually have nostrils, but the point is that even the divine, if it is to be to any extant comprehended by the human and certainly if it is to be perceived with immediacy, must be conveyed through the physical. This is another sense in which the psalms foretell the incarnation of Christ: if we are to know God, we must know God through flesh.

The Christian emphasis on embodiment finds its pinnacle in the incarnation of the second person of the Trinity. To atone for humanity's sin God must become man, and to become man God must be *made* flesh. We must not think of Jesus as a God *in* flesh. He is a God *of* flesh. John tells us not that "the Word disguised itself as flesh" or that "the Word hid in flesh" but that "the Word *became* flesh." Amidst controversy early in church history, regarding Christ's assumption of human nature, Gregory of Nazianzus asserted that, "For that which he has not assumed he has not healed; but that which is united to his Godhead is also saved. If only half Adam fell, then that which Christ assumes and saves may be half also; but if the whole of his nature fell, it must be united to the whole nature of Him that was begotten, and so be saved as a whole. Let them not, then, begrudge us our complete salvation, or clothe the Saviour only with bones and nerves and the portraiture of humanity."[7] Gregory insists that Christ doesn't just play dress-up in human shape but rather assumes a full humanity alongside his full divinity. He is not a God disguised as a human, as when Athena masquerades as Mentor or some other Greek in Homer's *Odyssey*. Nor is he an example of humanity merely possessed by deity, as when the Greeks thought Apollo spoke through an oracle at Delphi. Jesus is fully man and fully God. Orthodox Christianity insists upon this dual nature. This is the truth the ancient gnostics hated and the modern gnostics ignore.

And, as Gregory also insisted, he is flesh still.[8] Jesus did not rise as a ghost. He did not ascend into heaven as a spirit. The particularity of Christ Jesus demands in us a responding particularity. In one sense, at least, it is unchristian to generalize.

For that matter, we should recall that Jesus does not call out to his disciples like the ghost of old Hamlet to his son, "Remember me!" Instead, he gives them the bread and the wine. He says "*Do this* in remembrance of me." Our Lord links memory to matter and to action. He gives us the coarseness of bread, the taste of wine on which to rest our memories of him. Whatever

---

7. Gregory of Nazianzus, Epistle 101, in *Christology of the Later Fathers*, Hardy and Richardson, eds., 218–19.

8. Gregory of Nazianzus, Epistle 101, in *Christology of the Later Fathers*, Hardy and Richardson, eds., 218.

theological view one takes of communion, one must see that it involves a physical element. There can be no real "virtual" communion.

If our essential nature is in great part physical and if the central event of history—Christ's incarnation, crucifixion, and resurrection—is a matter of flesh, then we shouldn't be surprised that mere abstractions fail to move us. We shouldn't be surprised that the most powerful poems are the poems most rooted in physical reality. In Homer's great epics, rather than just being told about "the ocean" we are made to see "the wine dark sea." Shakespeare doesn't just tell us that he is balding, but rather, in his seventy-third sonnet, compares his head to "bare ruined choirs," the exposed remains of deserted monasteries. As many a middle-aged man can tell you, this is an image that brilliantly conveys the ruins of time in concrete form.

I do not mean that all abstraction is bad. Only that a good poem is anchored in concrete reality by means of definite imagery. As a general rule, the longer the poem the more abstraction it can bear. Eliot's *Four Quartets* or Stevens's "Notes Toward a Supreme Fiction," at many hundreds of lines, can get away with a great deal more abstraction than can a haiku in its tight three lines. The best haiku contain practically nothing but concrete imagery. A reader can tolerate some amount of abstraction, but only if the need for concrete particularity has first been met.

In his remarkable poem "Silt," Paul Mariani writes about facing his own mortality. Rather than saying something true but banal, such as "we all die someday," he puts us into the moment with striking images: "One morning you bend down to lace / your sneakers and find your leg stiff as a base- / ball bat."[9] The image places us firmly in our bodies, with not just an intellectual understanding of our, however distantly, impending death but also a physical realization of it. Later in the poem the "you" of the poem, whom one begins to suspect of being the poet, tells how his "poor leg whimpers for attention, until at last you get / the doctor, who finds a fourteen-inch blood clot / silting up your veins there on the sonar."[10] We will discuss the nearly magical power of metaphor in a later chapter. For now notice how much materiality the implied metaphors bring here in the form of the whimpering leg and the "silting" of veins like a river. Not only do we have the images implied in the metaphors, but also we can see the leg and the clot so much more clearly as themselves. Fittingly for a poem

---

9. Mariani, "Silt," in *Epitaphs for the Journey*, 145.
10. Mariani, "Silt," in *Epitaphs for the Journey*, 146.

about the inescapability of our physical death, the poem makes our sense of embodiment unavoidable.

To write *incarnationally* demands time and focus. Annie Finch, in her book *A Poet's Craft* says that "[o]ne of the great values of imagery in our time is that that it takes time. You are not likely to fill a poem with striking, moving images if you write it in harried haste, 'out of your head.' To notice imagery requires waiting: moving into the slowness of your senses and allowing sounds, smells, sights, touches, and tastes to well up in your awareness, to come to you."[11] Ultimately, then, failure to ground the poem in concrete reality is a failure of craftsmanship, a failure of patience, a failure of work ethic.

A powerful poem needs what T. S. Eliot calls an "objective correlative," by which he means an image that embodies, one might say *incarnates*, the feeling the poet wishes to convey.[12] Sometimes it is entirely explicable why a certain image conveys a certain feeling. Other times the connection is more mysterious, perhaps less objective than Eliot suggests. In her wonderful poem, "My Mother," for instance, Jane Kenyon perfectly embodies the childhood emotions of the speaker by presenting us with the material world as it meets the child's eye, describing particularly her mother's shoes and purse. When writing about one's mother, a writer might be tempted to offer little more than sentimental abstraction, but, recognizing that few relationships are as bodily real as that of a mother and the child she has given birth to and must keep alive day after day, Kenyon does not give in to this temptation. Instead, she focuses on small, specific details like the shoes with buttons that remind her of the eyes of fish, the thread in two different colors that her seamstress mother used in her work, her mother's big straw purse, and the common and familiar ball and paddle toy her mother brings home to her from a trip downtown. These concrete details so put us in the child's place, create such a sense of immediacy, that we are prepared to take in the poem's only abstraction in the surprising and powerful final line. If Kenyon had begun the poem with this line about her fear of abandonment, it would lack the punch it has following the accumulation of so much rich material detail.

Consider the physical detail packed into this short poem, also on the theme of the relationship between a mother and her daughter, by Jenny Yang Cropp:

11. Finch, *A Poet's Craft*, 130.
12. Eliot, "Hamlet and His Problems," in *Selected Essays*, 124–25.

> Her body squat, bent in thirds, grips
> the walls of a thick glass jar
> holding in the red heat, its pale
> veined leaves, fibrous cells beaten
> to agility by rock salt and rinsed
> clean to fit layer by layer. Between
> each, a thick coat of crushed peppers
> mixed into a paste. She won't tell me
> the other ingredients, refuses
> to let me come near enough, to see
> the small cracks in her hands,
> splits of skin in revolt. Instead, I hear
> the grunt and sigh of her work. Trial
> by raw flame. But we both know,
> have known from birth, to stuff the jar
> quietly, and not to flinch.[13]

Without saying anything directly on the subject, this poem speaks volumes about tradition, community, identity, womanhood, and the relationship between mothers and daughters. Images of food carry a particular weight in a poem, due to the way food functions as both a constant fact and a powerful symbol in all cultures. Like our Lord on the night before his crucifixion, Cropp embodies a big, almost unspeakable truth, in the tangible reality of a shared meal.

"No Ideas but in Things"

The only art in which I am competent is the making of poems, so I don't presume to say what would and would not constitute a Christianly embodiment in, say, painting or musical composition. I might, for instance, at first suspect that the painter in the realistic tradition has a better chance of avoiding creeping Gnosticism than does her sister the abstract expressionist. Then I remember, however, how certain abstract artists can focus us on the "thingness" of paint and the realness of color, and I am less sure in my pronouncement. I am not sure where one locates the particular in music, but I think I recognize it when I hear it. I believe it is possible for a

---

13. Cropp, "Watching my Mother Make Kimchi," in *String Theory*, 4.

composer to get the sound of a particular patch of earth into a piece of music. Certainly a great singer sings from his or her body as well as from the soul. All I can say for sure is that, whatever art form the Christian takes up, he should ask of his work, "where is the body?" and "Where is the earth?"

We don't feel in the heart what we can't see, touch, taste, or smell. Try thinking of your love for a person without thinking of that person's physical presence. Try thinking of your love for your husband or wife without thinking of the person himself or herself. To be honest, I am skeptical toward those who claim to fall in love online, but, even granted that it is possible, even online lovers tend to want to meet in person eventually. In fact, you should be highly suspicious if your digital lover doesn't want to meet in the flesh. Even leaving aside erotic desire, we cannot think of a loved one without picturing his or her physical reality. Long after they are gone, we may remember our parents' wisdom but we remember also, and perhaps more, their hands, their embraces, their physical presence in our lives. We long to be with those we love. We find greater happiness in proximity to our loved ones, even if it is just the child home from college sleeping in the next room. We desire to someday see our Jesus face to face.

"No ideas but in things," William Carlos Williams famously declared.[14] He was offering an assertion of imagist artistic doctrine, but he was also, if unaware, offering an assertion of orthodox Christian doctrine. That we are made from the dust of the earth is a biblical fact often raised as a reminder to humility, and rightly so. But is should also be a reminder of the goodness of materiality and of how thoroughly we are situated within the created, material world. Our humanity experiences itself within the context of the material. A poem that ignores this truth will never resonate deeply with a reader, because such a poem would be a lie about who we are.

---

14. Williams, *Paterson*, 14.

2

Diction

Words as Things

LIKE MANY PEOPLE OF a certain age, I learned much of what I know about language from *Sesame Street* and *The Electric Company*, thanks to countless hours in front of the television in the late '70s and early '80s. I remember well one frequent *Electric Company* skit, which was apparently called "Silhouette Blend." In this skit, two shadowed silhouettes faced each other, taking up most of the screen. One person would say the first part of a word, with the sound he is pronouncing emerging in written form from his lips. Then the other person would pronounce, and also physically emit in lexicographic form, the sounds to finish the word. As the two written halves of the word merged, the silhouetted couple would cheerily pronounce the whole word together.

What fascinated my childish mind about this skit was the way it treated sounds as if they were material *things*, like words were real objects. They seemed, in fact, almost more real than the shadowy people pronouncing them. Children instinctively grasp this thingness of words and treat bits of language like other fascinating objects they find, turning words over and over in their mouths the way they might turn a colorful and finely textured stone over and over in their hands—or, indeed, the way they might put such a stone into their mouths.

Years after leaving behind *The Electric Company*, when I was in college, I was again fascinated to discover a similar approach to the thingness of words in the great French poet Arthur Rimbaud's poem "Vowels," which begins "A noir, E blanc, I rouge, U vert, O bleu," or "A black, E white, I red, U green, O blue." The technical term for this sort of associative leaping from one kind of sense perception to another is *synesthesia*. A neuroscientist might consider this kind of perception the result of a crossed wire somewhere in the brain, but, for the poet, it is a condition that pushes the poem toward a more faithful depiction of the world.

As we have seen, concrete images help create aesthetically successful poems because they satisfyingly ground the poem in material creation. Images generally require several words to do this, functioning at the level of the phrase, clause, sentence, or even stanza. But another marker of a good poem is its ability to connect with the concrete world at the level of the single word. Good diction is incarnational diction.

Incarnational diction is difficult to achieve. In the age-old sibling rivalry between the arts, painters and sculptors seem to have an advantage over writers. When one works with paint or with metal to create a depiction of the concrete world, one is attempting to transform one *thing* into another *thing*. This is difficult, but it does not cross the unbridgeable boundary between *thing* and *not-thing*. When one is writing, however, one is attempting to create *thingness* out of something that is not, in the same sense, a *thing*. Perhaps only music has a larger gap to bridge. Poetry is a strange alchemy, most successful when stretching words into things which they are not.

The Diction Question

Words are perhaps not tangible things, but poets try to treat them as if they were. The mark of a real writer may just be a love of words as if they were real things in the created world, even if the writer's relationship with language is a vexed one due to the struggle of making real words behave as the writer wishes. We seem, however, often to misunderstand what it means to love words as part of God's creation. People who want to look smart love big, impressive, unusual words. Sometimes people who want to be thought poets pretend to love those flashy words as well. Real poets, however, love real words, the simple and powerful words of everyday speech. A real poet—that is, the person whose true vocation is the art of poetry—loves the words she is accustomed to tasting in her mouth. If one really loves language—if one loves one's own, particular language—then "blue" is as much a wonder and a gift as is "cerulean." Maybe it is more of a wonder, for it can do more things.

A Poetics of Orthodoxy

Much of modern literary history has been a war between "high" diction and "low" diction: the fancy words versus the regular, everyday words. At the end of the eighteenth century, in his preface to *The Lyrical Ballads*, William Wordsworth famously said, "I have proposed to myself to imitate, and as far as possible, to adopt, the very language of men."[1] To what extent Wordsworth was able to match his diction with that of the farmers and laborers he wrote about is debatable, but he clearly started English-language poetry in the aesthetic direction of pursuing regular speech, a rejection of the idea that there is a special "poetic diction" higher than and distinct from the everyday use of language. By the time we get to the twentieth century, even the flamboyant modernist, Ezra Pound, is advocating for a down-to-earth diction.[2] Today, most serious poets avoid "highfalutin'" language, unless they are using it to achieve a particular, often comic, effect. Certainly, unusual words have their place in poetry, but the widely shared consensus is that, on the whole, basic—if not necessarily rustic—diction is better.

Some Historical Considerations

The English language possesses an extraordinarily rich vocabulary, thanks to events in the early middle ages. When the French-speaking Normans invaded England in the eleventh century, their language was superimposed on the Germanic language of the dominant inhabitants (who had earlier invaded and driven speakers of Celtic languages, like Welsh, into the margins). As a result, modern English is a mishmash of French and a Germanic language usually referred to as "Old English" or "Anglo-Saxon." Sprinkled on top of that mixture is a fine layer of Latin, courtesy of the ubiquitous medieval church. Thus, English has several words for most things. One might speak of the *woods* or of the *forest*. If one is feeling very fancy, the adjective *sylvan* is also available, from the Latin.

For poetry written in English, a good basic rule is to go, whenever possible, with the Anglo-Saxon word. George Orwell made this one of his suggestions for good prose, suggesting that one should "[n]ever use a foreign phrase, a scientific word, or a jargon word if you can think of an everyday English equivalent."[3] Orwell complains that "[b]ad writers, and especially scientific, political, and sociological writers, are nearly always

---

1. Wordsworth, "Preface," in *The Lyrical Ballads*, 14.
2. Pound, *Literary Essays*, 5.
3. Orwell, "Politics and the English Language," in *The Orwell Reader*, 366.

DICTION

haunted by the notion that Latin or Greek words are grander than Saxon ones, and unnecessary words like *expedite, ameliorate, predict, extraneous, deracinated, clandestine, subaqueous,* and hundreds of others constantly gain ground from their Anglo-Saxon opposite numbers."[4] The tendency toward abstract and high diction is destructive of clarity in prose; in poetry it dilutes the emotional and sensory impact. Orwell had in mind particularly academic and political prose, but his rule is invaluable also in poetry, as every word choice is crucial in constructing a tight poem.

I often tell students that every line of a poem is a hallway the reader walks down. We want that hall to be lined with windows—the solid, vivid diction through which they can see—not with the thick, opaque doors of abstraction and dilution, through which they will be tempted to walk right out of the poem and find something better to do.

The good writer in English favors the vocabulary derived from Old English not out of some lingering resentment over the Norman Conquest, of course, but rather because these words are usually more visceral and natural to English speakers even today. The Old English words put less distance between the speaker/hearer and the real physical world. Because the Anglo-Saxon rooted word is often shorter, it is usually among the words we learn first. These words, it may just be, are survivors from our earliest days, a time when we lived more in our bodies and more in the material world, before we learned to retreat into abstractions. Thus, this basic vocabulary connects with us in a more "gut-level" way than does the French or Latin vocabulary. It is a very different thing to speak of the *domicile* you grew up in than it is to speak of the *house* in which you grew up. W. B. Yeats's great poem "Mad as the Mist and Snow" connects in a more visceral way with the reader than it would had he written a poem about how even the greatest minds of history were as "Insane as the Mist and Snow."[5] This verbal punch is caused in part by the elemental nature of the Old English vocabulary and in part by our tendency to use the Latinate vocabulary for technical purposes, leaving words like "insane" with a certain air of critical distance and clinical assessment about them. *Mad* takes us close to the point in a way that *insane* does not. One may speak of a *mad* cow, never, I think, of an *insane* one.

Clinical and Latinate terms have their place, of course, even in poetry. The late American poet John Ashbery was a master of using a distanced

---

4. Orwell, "Politics and the English Language," in *The Orwell Reader*, 358–59.
5. Yeats, "Mad as the Mist and Snow," in *The Collected Works*, 266.

vocabulary to create an acute sense of the loss of intimacy with the world and each other. Ashbery's use of multisyllabic and clinical words was an intentional irony. When, however, we rely too much on words like *insane*, we create a gnostic-like difference, a distance, between ourselves and the realities of the physical world. The poet, especially the Christian poet, should resist this distancing, even as the business-and-media-speak of our postmodern world rushes in the other, jargon- and argot-laden, direction.

Even more directly relevant to our concern to foster an incarnational vocabulary is the fact that, for English speakers, the Anglo-Saxon derived word often registers as more literal, more physically grounded, than does the French or Latinate word. When one goes to the *woods* one sees wood, if one speaks English. One would have to travel back through Old French to Latin in order to sees it as *forestis*, meaning something like "trees outside." If a shirt is *dirty* or *soiled,* one can see immediately what is on it. If the shirt is *sullied,* it is a rather more ambiguous matter. For the person rooted in the English language, the Old English vocabulary has built-in imagery; it is close to the material world as named in related words in the language. For the English-speaker, the basic English vocabulary is more incarnational. Or perhaps I should say that it is more *enfleshed.*

If you have read much modern poetry, you are probably familiar with William Carlos Williams's famous masterpiece of modernist minimalism, "The Red Wheel Barrow." This little poem is one of the most memorable poems of the twentieth century, and much of its impact is due to its simple and direct diction, words like *barrow, glazed, rain, water,* and *chickens*. Out of a few simple words Williams creates a vivid and strangely alluring masterpiece of compactness:

> so much depends
> upon
>
> a red wheel
> barrow
>
> glazed with rain
> water
>
> beside the white
> chickens[6]

6. Williams, "The Red Wheelbarrow," in *Selected Poems*, 56.

DICTION

Glazed, with its luxurious *z* sound, evokes a silky texture, and *chickens* is about as "chickeny" as a word can be (I find it impossible to pronounce the word *chicken* without at least slightly bobbing my head in a most chicken-like way). This brief poem almost entirely avoids words that might create distance between it and the physical world. The poem's only goal seems to be to bring us close to the physical world, to make us note what *is,* and any fancy words would certainly distract from that aim.

For a contrast, consider the following bad poem:

> A multitude is contingently
> Associated with
> A traditional, mono-wheeled agricultural
> Conveyance
> Dampened with recent
> Precipitation
> In proximity to the alabaster
> *Gallus gallus domesticus.*

Nearly every word in this poem seems to move us further away from physical reality. This poem might amuse us by inviting us into the world of language, but it never connects that world to the real world, and thus fails to honor the gift of both word and world. It lacks punch because it lacks flesh. The original poem, regardless of one's opinions on the merits or demerits of free verse, is one of the most memorable poems of the twentieth century, yet the decomposed version is entirely forgettable. The false poem never lands on a visceral, physical level. It never directs our attention to the *being* of the world, which in turn would ultimately direct our attention to the *Being* who is its creator.

Of course, one should not be legalistic about diction. I am not recommending setting up some sort of "Anglo-Saxon only" rule as the poetic equivalent of a King James-only stance on translations of the Bible. French and Latinate words can be useful and perfectly appropriate, as long as each word is carefully weighed before being employed.

Nor am I generally disparaging the Latin language itself. I am a proponent of classical education, and I think every person could benefit from the study of Latin. Latin is a beautiful and useful language, and I have fallen in love with much ancient Roman poetry, such as the words of Virgil's Aeneas in book one of the *Aeneid*. Viewing the story of the fall of Troy depicted on a temple of Juno, Aeneas sighs out, *sunt lacrimae rerum,* "these are the tears of things." This is a beautiful lament, and it sounds like weeping when pronounced, to the best of our knowledge, as an ancient Roman would pronounce it. To insist on the more visceral word in English-language poetry isn't to diminish Virgil's accomplishment in Latin but rather to honor it by trying to approach it in the language we write in and speak in every day.

Also, the poet working in English now has a globe's worth of vocabulary to draw from, as our language continues to be enriched by interaction with other languages. Just as useful as the Anglo-Saxon words to the Anglophone poet are the words of his or her particular region and heritage. When Filipino-American poet, Janine Joseph, refers to her grandparents as *Abu* and *Aba* throughout her book, *Driving without a License*, we can feel her own intimacy with the words.[7] Similarly, when Ron Wallace, in his wonderful poem "Learning to Speak Choctaw," uses *Halito* and *Yokoke*, not only is it clear from the context that the words mean "Hello" and "thank you," but also it is striking how much depth and resonance they add to the conversation in the poem.[8] Perhaps the best way to keep poetic language out of gnostic abstraction is for the poet to use the words of which he feels the most ownership. The thesaurus is a great tool for writing term papers, but it leads to a disconnected, gnostic diction in poetry. A poet should never use a word he or she doesn't in some real way "own" or, better yet, "belong to."

Playing with Sound

Another way in which good poetry can close the gap between words and the world is through the use of sound. Of course, if words can be said to have any actual physical existence it is in the vibration of the human vocal chords and the interaction of tongue, teeth, and lips. Sometimes, the particular way in which a word is articulated gives it a particular closeness to the material world. In other words, attention to the sounds of words reinforces the thingness of words. Contemporary American poet Mark Doty links this physicality of words to gratitude for the given physical world. He writes, "Sonic texture can itself be a form of praise, a kind of savoring of things. When Galway Kinnell speaks of 'the long, perfect loveliness of sow' he wants us to feel the mouth-resonance of those *o's—long, love, sow* —elongating the *o* in long, holding it against the shorter *o* of *love*, then the

---

7. Joseph, *Driving without a License*.
8. Wallace, "Learning to Speak Choctaw," in Brown, ed., *Oklahoma Poems*, 23.

deeper vibration of *sow*, so that the soughing and roundness of the vowels themselves become a kind of parallel text to the creature herself, stating an emotional position toward her, physically fulfilling or demonstrating the pleasure and blessing the poem describes."[9] For Doty, savoring words is savoring the world, an impulse he links directly to the childish desire to put the whole world in one's mouth. The truth of his view is easily demonstrated when one spends a few minutes with small children. My own children have often driven my wife and I to distraction with repeating words that they have discovered feel good in their mouths. Kids have an instinct for noticing the buttery texture of a word like *peanut butter* and should be encouraged to give thanks for the gifts of sound and language.

Great children's books are full of wonderful sound. Though nothing could conquer my three children's hatred of bedtime, I always felt that Margaret Wise Brown's classic *Goodnight, Moon*, with its deep "o" sounds and its lush "sh" sounds, at least helped a bit. As in the line from Kinnell which Doty quotes, in Brown's book low vowels do a lot of good work, creating a sense of peace, quiet, and heavy sleepiness. The combination of *sh* with all the deep *o* and *u* sounds is a delicious glass of warm milk (or chamomile tea, if that makes you less queasy). By way of contrast, imagine the effect of this hypothetical Australian version:

> G'night stick
> G'night snake
> G'night brick
> G'night mate
> And g'night to Mick grilling steak.

The high i sounds create a completely different tone and experience than do Brown's deep o's. The low sounds of the original are lulling, suggestive of deepness, solemnity, and slow movement. The high vowel sounds of my version suggest rather quickness, smallness, and energy. The hypothetical Australian version is hardly the stuff of bedtime reading.

Vowel sounds interact with the physical world in ways that are both strange and universally recognized. If I tell you I have two friends named Bubba and Peewee, you will make certain assumptions about the physicality of both men, provided we have not wandered into the territory of ironic nicknames. In the classic poetry textbook, *The Western Wind*, one finds a very handy chart arranging vowel sounds from the low *boo* to the high

---

9. Doty, *Art of Description*, 120.

bee.[10] Lower vowels like *o* and *u* slow down a line of poetry, and, depending on other factors like diction and imagery, give the line a mood ranging from melancholy to peaceful. Alternately, lots of high vowels, like *i* and *e*, tend to speed the line up and give an impression of lightness and energy. When Shakespeare, counting up his sorrows in his thirtieth sonnet, tells how he is wont to "heavily from woe to woe tell o'er / The sad account of fore-bemoaned moan," it is in large part those deep *o* sounds that make us feel the weight of his sad reckoning.[11]

Master poets manipulate sound to create mood and augment images. Consider, for example, how John Milton affects a shift in dominant vowel sounds to signal a shift in mood at the beginning of his hymn to happiness "L'Allegro":

> Hence loathed Melancholy
> Of *Cerberus* and blackest midnight born,
> In *Stygian* Cave forlorn
> 'Mongst horrid shapes, and shrieks, and sights unholy,
> Find out some uncouth cell,
> Where brooding darkness spreads his jealous wings,
> And the night-Raven sings;
> There under *Ebon* shades, and low-brow'd Rocks,
> As ragged as thy Locks,
> In dark *Cimmerian* desert ever dwell.
> But come thou Goddess fair and free,
> In Heav'n yclep'd *Euphrosyne*,
> And by me, heart-easing Mirth,
> Whom lovely *Venus* at a birth
> With two sisters Graces more
> To Ivy-crowned *Bacchus* bore.[12]

Notice how the dominant vowel sounds change from low to high when the poet has banished melancholy and welcomed mirth. Of course, one can find high vowels and low vowels throughout the poem, but a certain register of vowel clearly dominates most lines, contributing significantly to their pace and their tone. For an expert poet like Milton, words are more than

---

10. Nims and Mason, *Western Wind*, 154–55.
11. Shakespeare, Sonnet #130, in *The Riverside Shakespeare*, 1754–55.
12. Milton, "L'Allegro," in *Complete Poems*.

DICTION

transparent vessels for meaning; they are things themselves and interact with the world in almost physical ways.

Of course, close attention to vowels should accompany the cultivation of consonants. The authors of *The Western Wind* call our attention to the way Yeats creates a "liquid" sound through the alliteration in this line from "The Lake Isle of Innisfree": "I hear lake water lapping with low sounds by the shore[.]"[13] Despite his own heterodox, spiritualist beliefs, "incarnational" seems to me the best way to sum up Yeats's accomplishment in bringing the sound of words so close to the sound of the world.

For another example, read Robert Frost's sonnet, "The Oven Bird," aloud and listen to the interplay of vowel, consonant, and metrical stress:

> There is a singer everyone has heard,
> Loud, a mid-summer and a mid-wood bird,
> Who makes the solid tree trunks sound again.
> He says that leaves are old and that for flowers
> Mid-summer is to spring as one to ten.
> He says the early petal-fall is past
> When pear and cherry bloom went down in showers
> On sunny days a moment overcast;
> And comes that other fall we name the fall.
> He says the highway dust is over all.
> The bird would cease and be as other birds
> But that he knows in singing not to sing.
> The question that he frames in all but words
> Is what to make of a diminished thing.[14]

When Frost describes the oven bird as "a mid-summer and a mid-wood bird," all those *d* sounds somehow give the impression of woodiness. Frost reinforces this impression in the next line using metrical substitution (stressed syllables where we would expect unstressed ones) along with the alliteration of "t" sounds: "Who makes the solid tree trunks sound again." These effects in combination with the rhyme and meter of the poem create a deeply satisfying encounter with words, an encounter that is also with the physical world.

---

13. Nims and Mason, *Western Wind*, 164.
14. Frost, "The Oven Bird," in *Poetry of Robert Frost*, 119.

A Poetics of Orthodoxy

Enfleshed Language

Some poets—such as the great seventeenth-century, English, Christian poet George Herbert—have sought ways to push the incarnation of language even further. Although back in elementary school, you may have written poems in the shape of roller skates or kites, Herbert's shape poems, "The Altar" and "Easter Wings," in which the shape of the words on the page suggest the object after which the poems are named, are not just seventeenth-century school projects. They are attempts to bridge the gap between words and things, and in that an attempt to echo Jesus's bridging of the gap between God and man. Herbert takes "the word became flesh" as the heart not only of his theology but also of his aesthetics:

> Lord, who createdst man in wealth and store,
>   Though foolishly he lost the same,
>   Decaying more and more,
>   Till he became
>   Most poore:
>   With thee
>   O let me rise
>   As larks, harmoniously,
> And sing this day thy victories:
> Then shall the fall further the flight in me.
>
> My tender age in sorrow did beginne
>   And still with sicknesses and shame.
>   Thou didst so punish sinne,
>   That I became
>   Most thinne.
>   With thee
>   Let me combine,
>   And feel thy victorie:
> For, if I imp my wing on thine,
> Affliction shall advance the flight in me.[15]

Most obviously, the poem, when turned on its side, resembles two pairs of angels' wings. This is a clear effort to bridge the gap between word and

---

15. Herbert, "Easter-Wings," in *Works of George Herbert*, 43.

world. More subtly, the number of syllables in each line grows less as the speaker grows more spiritually poor, down to one two-syllable foot at "Most poore" in the first stanza and "Most thinne" in the second. Yet each shortest line is matched with a "With thee," to embody the love of the God who embodies himself to meet us at our most spiritually poor. When we are at our least, we meet him who humbled himself for us. Herbert's poem brilliantly attempts to incarnate incarnation.

Few poets will go as far as Herbert, and few have the musical ear of Shakespeare or Yeats or Frost, but all good poetry strives toward uniting words and the world. A true poem happens when poets attempt to be like those silhouetted faces on *The Electric Company*, pushing words from our lips into the physical universe. Such a poetic act imitates and honors the God who spoke the world into existence, just as the effort to overcome the distance between word and world honors the Word who became flesh and dwelt among us.

3

The Sentimentality Trap

How Much Emotion?

SENTIMENTALITY IS THE AESTHETIC sin that so easily besets Christian art. The Christian artists, in as much as he seeks an audience within the church, will be constantly tempted toward the sentimental. But what do we mean when we describe a work of art as "sentimental"?

I wish to stress from the beginning of this chapter that sentimentality is not simply too much emotion, but rather an imbalance of emotion, an over-investment of emotion relative to that in which it is invested. Sentimentality is a misdirection of emotion, emotion for its own sake without a reference in the tangible world. Rejecting sentimentality does not mean rejecting emotion as a fundamental part of aesthetic experience. I have never put down a poem and complained that it was too moving, too resonant. Sentimentality, on the other hand, I find immediately repulsive.

In seeking to reject the sentimental, it is certainly all too easy to overcorrect. T. S. Eliot once claimed that "Poetry is not a turning loose of emotion, but an escape from emotion."[1] Fortunately, he did not follow this prescription too scrupulously in his own poems, and even *The Wasteland* includes a touching personal reference to his nervous breakdown. Such an attitude toward emotion is, I suspect, a legacy of the influence of logical positivist philosophy upon modernist poetry. The positivists, who had

---

1. Eliot, "Tradition and the Individual Talent," in *Selected Essays*, 10.

great influence in the twentieth century, argued that the only worthwhile form of knowledge is analytical and empirical knowledge, what is directly provable. It is an attitude that is distrustful of human feeling not for the Christian reasons—that the heart is wicked and feeling can be misleading—but rather merely because feeling is not fact, is not scientific.

Such an attitude toward feeling is a slippery slope that leads to less and less emotion in poetry, for if feeling itself is the problem, then obviously the less feelings in a poem, the better. The end result is the sort of avant-garde poem that offers a random series of letters and numbers as poetry, as in much of the work of Charles Bernstein and the so-called "L=A=N=G=U=A=G=E poets," a kind of poem I find about as engaging and meaningful as, well, a random series of letters and numbers. This is a kind of "experimental" work that Eliot himself had the moderation and good sense to avoid. Such work isn't sentimental, but I also have a hard time calling it poetry.

What is Sentimentality?

Sentimentality is a defect in the quality, not the quantity, of feeling in a poem. But how is a writer or a reader to recognize this defect in feeling that we are calling sentimentality? The best guide is wide experience of the art. The great tradition is a highly reliable guide in this matter, and, reading those poets we have, by an election lasting generations, inducted into the canon, one finds very little that is sentimental. Millennia before sentimentality was given a name in the eighteenth century and elevated to prominence in popular literature, the imbalance between emotion and its object was resisted in the sober wisdom of Homer and the tragic vision of Virgil. Long before critics and philosophers of aesthetics defined sentimentality, it was rebuked in the frank self-evaluation of John Donne's devotional poems, his honesty about his own weakness and sin.

Another great poet, Gerard Manley Hopkins, working in the nineteenth century, an age in which sentimentality enjoyed a great vogue, often approaches the sentimental but stops short of indulging in it, as in the stark and restrained closing lines of the "terrible sonnet" usually referred to as "Carrion Comfort": "Cheer whom though? The hero whose heaven-handling flung me, foot trod / Me? or me that fought him? O which one? is it each one? That night, that year / Of now done darkness I wretch lay wrestling with (my God!) my God."[2] There is here none of the pharisaical self-righteousness that one finds in so much Christian sentimentality. Rather, Hopkins gives a frank, unflinching, and unexaggerated account of his spiritual struggles. The poet's restraint puts parentheses around the exclamation, a device that prevents the awe from disproportionately ruling the line. With the emotion in proper proportion, we do not lose sight of the physical reality behind the poem, a reality subtly conveyed in the verb *lay*. The specificity of the verb gives us a glimpse of a real man passing sleepless nights upon his cot. It is clear that Hopkins learned much of his craft from reading the Psalms. The poem, though focused on spiritual struggle, is far from abstract sentimentality.

The wrongness of sentimentality comes in inverse proportion to the rightness of the kinds of concrete images and diction we discussed in the previous two chapters. In, to take another example which I encourage you to read for yourself, T. S. Eliot's "Ash Wednesday" the emotion resides in the images, strange and evocative, rather than in abstractions overlaid them like a cheap enamel. The poem is spiritually serious and, despite Eliot's warning about emotion, profoundly moving, but there is not a trace of sentimentality in it. Rather, there is real feeling attached to the real world, the world of both spiritual and physical reality.[3]

The best education in reading and in writing is reading. If one develops a familiarity with great poetry, which is almost never sentimental, one will find that sentimentality is simply no longer satisfying. Once one knows the real thing, the artificial substitute no longer will do.

Sentimentality and Pornography

The problem with sentimentality is that it offers us the dubious chance to feel, while bypassing the messiness of any real human engagement: not too much feeling but too thin an experience. This is what the great southern novelist Flannery O'Connor meant when she wrote, "We lost our innocence in the Fall, and our return to it is through the Redemption which was brought about by Christ's death and by our slow participation in it. Sentimentality is a skipping of this process in its concrete reality and an early arrival at a mock state of innocence, which strongly suggests its opposite. Pornography . . . is essentially sentimental, for it leaves out the connection

---

2. Hopkins, "Carrion Comfort," in *Major Works*, 168.
3. Eliot, "Ash Wednesday," in *Poems of T. S. Eliot*.

of sex with its hard purpose, and so far disconnects it from its meaning in life as to make it simply an experience for its own sake."[4] Sentimentality is emotional satisfaction without emotional connection, an agreement between the artist and the audience to skip straight to the gratification, which, due to the skipping, is not so gratifying after all—as Shakespeare knowingly suggests in his Sonnet 129 ("Th' expense of spirit in a waste of shame"). That is why O'Connor links it to pornography.

The popular painter Thomas Kinkade's cozy little cottages, for instance, offer all the warmth of home—something I certainly enjoy—but what is the warmth of home without knowing the coldness of the world? What is homecoming without the hard journey? In Hebrews, we read that "These all died in faith, not having received the things promised, but having seen them and greeted them from afar, and having acknowledged that they were strangers and exiles on the earth. For people who speak thus make it clear that they are seeking a homeland" (11:13–14). We are at home on the earth, which is God's creation, and not at home on the earth, which is cursed by our fall. To live in this tension is to live in the truth, and even the reader who knows nothing of Christianity's emphasis on the *in-betweeness* of present human existence will feel that reality has been missed when the search for a country has been omitted from a work of art. Kinkade's error is not in depicting the homecoming; it is in ignoring the seeking. That is why, when a student told me that she lovingly sends a Kinkade postcard to her grandmother once a month, I blurted, "Stop sending pornography to your grandma!" Art must be truthful in what it says about the world and our sojourn in it. Lying down in green pastures is a great goal for an artist, but he must not attempt to get there without walking through the valley of the shadow of death. If he does, he is a liar.

Sentimentality is really yet another form of that deadly heresy of Gnosticism, which prefers airy spiritualization to God's actual creation. Christian sentimentality wants to transcend the material reality of the world, gesturing toward it only with stock abstractions—Grandma's hands, baby feet, home sweet home—that have no correspondence with the actual physical world, in order to get to a prearranged rendezvous of feeling. Like the gnostic, the sentimentalist denies the incarnation. This denial comes most often in the form of a blindness to the particularity of creation, the same kind of blindness that has burdened so many of our Sunday school classroom walls with a generalized, handsome, and Teutonic Jesus when in

---

4. O'Connor, *Mystery and Manners*, 148.

fact our Lord was and is no doubt far more Semitic, and probably rugged, in his actual appearance. In other words, the problem with poems about "Grandma's hands" is not the subject matter *per se* but rather that the creator of such a poem has little regard for the actual hands of the lady in question. The woman's body parts are turned into cheap vehicles for cheap spiritual gratification, a kind of pornography.

The same is true of poems about "baby feet" and "innocent smiles" and any such stock image. Such poems ignore the state of actual, particular children in the world. Perhaps even worse, they cover up even the existence of particular children, real beings in possession of both the *imago Dei* and fallen human nature. I sometimes think any Christian poet caught blathering about "the innocence of childhood" should be forced to read St. Augustine's *Confessions* and made to work twenty hours in the church nursery. Anyone caught posting such a poem on the church bulletin board should be assigned to monitor the fourth-grade boys' Sunday school class.

Sentimentality and Contemporary Poetry

Sentimentality is a temptation not just for those working within the church. Sentimentality is the sin that so easily besets the new group of poets often referred to as "instapoets," after the medium, Instagram, through which they share their work. The most prominent of these poets are Tyler Knott Gregson and Rupi Kaur, and their work has now made its way from the internet into big-box bookstores around the country.[5] Many contemporary poets and critics feel that the instapoets write badly, but secular aesthetics is somewhat at a loss when it comes to justifying that opinion, unable as postmodern aesthetics are to ground its judgments in anything deeper or larger than personal preference. Without a grounding metaphysic, what can the defender of literary values say of the instapoet other than a general charge of being naïve, or, in other words, of being unhip?

On the other hand, the defenders of the instapoets are apt to say that just being popular does not make the instapoets' poems bad. That is true enough. Both Byron and Tennyson managed, despite a great amount of fame and rock star-like attention, to write poems that will be read for as long as poetry is savored.

---

5. Alter, "Web Poets' Society," 1.

The Sentimentality Trap

I am afraid, however, that being bad is exactly what has made the poems of the instapoets popular.[6] Like pornography, sentimentality avoids engagement with real emotion or relationships and goes instead for cheap feeling, an approach that flatters readers with the perceived correctness of their sentiments. Both pornography and Gnosticism tend to feed narcissism. It is no wonder that such poetry has wide appeal in an age in which we have elevated "self-esteem" above the classical virtues of self-sacrifice and nobility.

Of course, the problem with instapoetry is not sentiment but sentimentality. One may read many poems on Instagram about the purported resilience, emotional and physical, of the poet, the "I never give up" theme being a go-to for these poets. This is not a bad theme; it was, after all, good enough for Homer and his *Odyssey*. But it is rarely handled well by these poets. For contrast, visit the Instagram account of Tyler Knott Gregson and read the poem that begins with the line "I kept going," and then consider this simple and beautiful poem about perseverance by the great Langston Hughes:

> Well, son, I'll tell you:
> Life for me ain't been no crystal stair.
> It's had tacks in it,
> And splinters,
> And boards torn up,
> And places with no carpet on the floor –
> Bare.
> But all the time
> I'se been a climbin' on,
> And reachin' landin's,
> And turnin' corners,
> And sometimes goin' in the dark
> Where there ain't been no light.
> So boy, don't you turn back.
> Don't you set down on the steps
> 'Cause you find it's kinder hard.
> Don't you fall now—

---

6. I base this opinion in part on the "undercover" work of Andrew Lloyd, for *Vice*, who intentionally wrote the worst poems he could and saw his Instagram account flourish as a result. See Lloyd, "I Faked my Way."

> For I'se still goin', honey,
> I'se still climbin',
> And life for me ain't been no crystal stair.[7]

Notice how Hughes's poem works in the exact opposite direction from the abstract and self-obsessed poetry of Gregson. Hughes looks toward others and toward the physical world. Hughes follows his speaker's metaphor to concentrate a lifetime of challenges into a clear picture that keeps us grounded in physical reality. Notice, too, that Hughes puts all the wisdom in the mouth of somebody else. He rejects the temptation to make himself the hero of his own poem and thus escapes the gnostic sentimentality of self-congratulation that plagues Gregson's poems and instapoetry in general.

The poetry of Robert Frost, also, provides a bracing antidote to sentimentality, even when he is addressing topics often sentimentalized, as in his wonderful poem "Birches." Though Frost is writing about boyhood, the art of tree climbing, and the human desire for heaven, he avoids all traces of sentimentality. The poem in is not only one of the finest poems in the English language but is also a wonderful meditation on the in-betweeness that characterizes the life of the believer. The poem starts out simply:

> When I see birches bend to left and right
> Across the lines of straighter darker trees,
> I like to think some boy's been swinging them.
> But swinging doesn't bend them down to stay.
> Ice-storms do that.[8]

Already the poet is revising himself, checking his own impulse to romanticize his encounter with both the natural world and his own nostalgia. This is the kind of sobriety of thought that marks all of Frost's great poems and that has given him a reputation for wisdom.

The poem goes on to offer a series of powerful and particular images that situate the joy of the "swinger of birches" within the real and fallen world: ice like broken glass, trees bent by weather, a face that "burns and tickles with the cobwebs / Broken across it," and an eye watering "From a twig's having lashed across it open." The poem is full of images of brokenness but also of great beauty. Even while offering such vivid and compelling images, the speaker continues to correct and second-guess himself throughout, the poem's wisdom becoming all the more convincing because

---

7. Hughes, "Mother to Son," in *Selected Poems*, 187.
8. Frost, "Birches," in *Poetry of Robert Frost*, 121–22.

it doesn't boast of itself. Such wisdom seems hard-earned in one sense, but, in another sense it seems to be given to the speaker rather than earned at all. The speaker in Frost's poem yearns, as he says, "*Toward* heaven." He does not give us the impression that he and I are exactly the kind of people who reach heaven easily or have in fact already found it here on earth, a move too often made in much contemporary "nature writing." Inasmuch as Frost's poem idealizes childhood—which, the poet admits, can be very lonely—it does so only as a paradise lost, something the poet clearly can access now only through memory. Frost's poem presents a grown person in a real world, a person thinking fondly, even longingly of childhood but without any Peter Pan delusions. The quiet understatement of the final line—"Once could do worse than be a swinger of birches"—tops it all off exceptionally well.

Our Sentimental Age

Sentimentality abounds perhaps especially in American Christian culture and saturates the reading done by American Christians. Sentimentality is no doubt one aspect of the more general superficiality of our cultural moment in and outside of the church. Many prominent publishers of Christian books offer extensive lines of novels in the "Amish romance" genre as well as an endless supply of spiritually tinted self-help books but little in terms of Christian classics and no poetry in a contemporary vein. Christian booksellers sometimes offer the poetry of Amy Carmichael, whose life and work certainly inspire but whose verse is flat and sugary, but they sell nothing from contemporary poetry's most prominent Christian poets, such as Denise Levertov, Richard Wilbur, and Mark Jarman. As Todd Brenneman argues in his recent book, *Homespun Gospel: The Triumph of Sentimentality in Contemporary American Evangelicalism*, sentimentality may be a defining characteristic of religious life for many Americans, and so most readers in the dominant evangelical culture, outside of a few hip and urban churches, are more likely to encounter the treacly poetry of Ruth Bell Graham than the spiritually searing work of R. S. Thomas or T. S. Eliot.[9]

Why are so many Christian writers and readers drawn to sentimentality? Why is it that if one Googles the phrase "Christian poetry" one has to wade through pages of results with titles like "Grandma's Praying Hands" and "Childhood Smiles" before getting to Dante, George Herbert, and Paul

9. Brenneman, *Homespun Gospel*.

Mariani? I suspect it has to do with a misguided interpretation of the verse with which I began this book, Philippians 4:8, "Finally, brothers, whatever is true, whatever is honorable, whatever is just, whatever is pure, whatever is lovely, whatever is commendable, if there is any excellence, if there is anything worthy of praise, think about these things." This verse is often evoked in admonition to avoid the garbage of popular entertainment, and rightly so. Pursuing what is lovely should leave no room in our life for cultivating the spiritual and ethical ugliness of much of our popular culture. But the verse should also be taken as a call to pursue closeness to God by seeking out and cherishing truth, goodness, and beauty. The Philippians 4:8 way of life does not mean that we should model our mental and emotional lives on those three monkeys who hear no evil, see no evil, and speak no evil. Unfortunately, forgetting the apostle's direction toward honesty, many Christians seem to believe that what Scripture means by "pure" and by "lovely" is merely the pleasant and the naive, the Hallmark Channel, not the reality of a world in need of redemption.

Yet, looked at through the initially disorienting but ultimately corrective lens of Scripture itself, what is more pure and lovely than the cross? One might answer, "the resurrection," but there is no resurrection without crucifixion. The Christian sentimentalist wants the bliss of Easter morning without the pain of Good Friday or the sorrow of Holy Saturday, reducing the great joy of Easter to the pleasantness of a watercolor sunrise on a greeting card. The sacrifice of our savior is lovely. His blood is pure. If we can look on these things and know they are good, then we, in a deeply Christian art, should not fear looking at the hard realities of our fallen world. Dostoevsky has demonstrated this principle clearly with novels like *Crime and Punishment*. The Christian artist who wraps himself in sunbeams and daffodils fails to be Christian at all, producing a bloodless, lifeless art that pleases a middle-class consumerism or a postmodern self-esteem, not an authentic Christian encounter with a hurting world.

We often see sentimentality take the form of attempts to make the Cross agreeable and respectable. This is the attempted domestication of the scandal of God's death for us, accomplished by the fad of sticking the Cross onto handbags and the back pockets of jeans. The tendency is at least as old as the nineteenth-century American "fireside poet" John Greenleaf Whittier, whose "The Crucifixion" makes much of seeing "the suffering son of God" but never shows us any concrete bodily suffering. Whittier begins with a postcard from the holy land:

The Sentimentality Trap

> Sunlight upon Judaea's hills!
> And on the waves of Galilee;
> On Jordan's stream, and on the rills
> That feed the dead and sleeping sea!
> Most freshly from the green wood springs
> The light breeze on its scented wings;
> And gayly quiver in the sun
> The cedar tops of Lebanon![10]

This is a lively opening with several lovely images, but unfortunately, the poem over-stretches the moment and maintains this postcard-picturesque tone throughout. It insists on the dramatic difference made by the crucifixion but fails to notice the actual man on the cross. Instead, we have abstract gestures toward it in phrases such as "That Sacrifice!—the death of Him,— / The Christ of God, the holy One!" The lack of concrete reality is implicitly admitted by the exclamation marks, mere stage directions to tell us how to feel. This is a plastic crucifixion aimed to elicit an instant emotional response, which produces in readers nothing much deeper than self-satisfaction as they arrive at it. Contrast Whittier's relatively bloodless Christ with the powerful tradition of the *ecce homo* ("behold the man") in Christian painting, and you will understand what is missing from the poem. Consider, for instance, the thin and awkwardly bound Jesus of Caravaggio's 1605 *Ecce Homo* or the thorn-crowned and dazed Christ of Cigoli's 1607 *Ecce Homo*.

The failure of Whittier's exclamation marks shows clearly by contrast with wholly unsentimental poetic treatments of the crucifixion as well. John Poch's "The Cross," from his 2009 collection *Dolls*, is a splendid example of addressing the cross without a hint of sentimentality. The poem begins with images of the body:

> You can make one with your fingers,
> your hands, your whole body.
> A common tattoo.
> A corkscrew gone through itself,
> away from the wine and into the hand.[11]

By moving the piercing of the hand out of the expected context and thus removing the conventional emotional cues, Poch makes the pain seem real again. One can't read the lines without thinking about the pierced hand as

---

10. Whittier, "The Crucifixion," in *Poems of Whittier*, 309–10.
11. Poch, "The Cross," in *Dolls*, 37.

a real hand really pierced. One thinks of one's own hands along with the hands of Christ. Because of that, one thinks of God truly incarnate. The difference between Whittier's version and Poch's version is not the subject matter, which is nearly identical, nor is it the *amount* of emotion, but rather the authenticity of the feeling, a freshness achieved by avoiding anything like automatic emotion evoked by conventional signs for "insert appropriate feeling here." It is an authenticity achieved by a willingness to imagine the particular, the unique, the real, the actual body of our savior and—as later in the poem he calls our attention to "a million potential splinters"—the actual cross of wood on which he hanged.

Walking a Fine Line

In my introductory poetry workshop, I find I need to discourage half the class from writing about puppies, rainbows, and Grandmother's praying hands, but another kind of sentimentality also threatens. It turns away from Hallmark naivete, but then cultivates the stereotypical gritty irony of the television cop program, second-rate punk rock, or hackneyed attempts at film noir. Thus I have to steer the other half of the class away from an equal and opposite form of sentimentality. These students, raised on *The Hunger Games* and postmodern hip, fill their poems with broken glass and the smell of urine in alleyways. Surprisingly, there is really very little difference between the two tones; both are shortcuts and generalizations. Neither version, one a stock sentimentality and the other its snit-sentimental mirror image, is truly incarnational; both are comprised of commonplace images only seemingly aimed at the actual world.

Given the choice, I suppose I would prefer to read a student's version of Baudelaire rather than of Swinburne, but both are failures of art, failures at creation. The writer, especially the Christian, is today as obligated to avoid the sentimental anti-sentimentality of the edgy as he is to avoid puppies and Pollyanna. Both reflect shoddy workmanship. Both are cheap goods made cheaply.

But should we insist on well-made things, on bespoke poems that might be "beyond the masses"? It has sometimes been suggested to me that my position on sentimentality might be "elitist," and, if by "elitist" we mean only, as is sometimes the case, the preference for things that are better over things that are inferior, then I am guilty as charged. It is, after all, my project in this book to argue for the preference of some poems over others.

The Sentimentality Trap

What people usually seem to mean by *elitism*, however, is mere snobbery, looking down on an entire class of people for their membership in that class. In that case, it seems to me that it is rather more elitist to suggest that the masses are incapable of appreciating better art than it is to insist that they have a chance to appreciate something finer. Isn't it more "elitist" to keep Bach to myself while smiling patronizingly at the unwashed and their pop music than it is to take the time to introduce my neighbor to better music? It is the exact inverse of snobbery to suggest that the average man or women on the street, or in the pews, is fully capable of enjoying an aesthetic experience superior to mass-produced sentimental dreck.

I come from a long line of oil field workers and farmers. My father had only a high school education and, through long bouts of unemployment, often took odd jobs to make ends meet. In short, I come from the very "*hoi polloi*"—around here we're just called "rednecks"—that some would suggest are incapable of eating solid intellectual and spiritual food, and, having spent my life among rural working people, I can assure you that we are as capable of reading Dostoevsky (whom I discovered on my father's bookshelf) as we are of reading *Chicken Soup for the Soul*. If the latter is more often the fare we are discovered eating, that is because it is all too often the only food we have been offered.

The Apostle Paul suggests that some can only digest milk, but he says this is because they are "not *yet* ready" for solid food. The very purpose of his epistle is to goad them toward better fare. The failure to "put away childish things" can, in its extreme, be a form of perversion and is not a way of life the thoughtful Christian should encourage for anyone.

If followed to its logical conclusion, the idea that we should just lighten up and let the masses have their sentimentality contributes to the push to remove consideration of the true, the good, and the beautiful from our schools and colleges. Why teach Beethoven to our fifth-grade music students? Just have them sing some Beatles songs, and "Let [them] be." Or, better yet, get rid of music all together: they can spend more time in "STEM" classes. Why keep that difficult, elitist old Shakespeare around our state schools and community colleges? Television studies for all!

It is not an enforcement of Spartan toughness upon the average reader to suggest that he or she eschew sentimentality, as the rejection of sentimentality is not the rejection of emotion itself. It is, rather, an invitation to a more sumptuous and nourishing feast. There is nothing "elitist" in wishing all people access to truly great art anymore than there would be something "elitist" in wishing all people access to healthy, nourishing, and delicious food. The human soul is the same, educated elite or *hoi polloi*, and it, despite all its corruption, is nobly made. I would no sooner let be a soul drowning in kitsch than I would let be a man on a sinking raft.

Don't get me wrong. I agree with Ted Kooser, who argues in his excellent *Poetry Home Repair Manual* that it is far better to risk being sentimental than it is to accept a dry, emotionless kind of poetry.[12] I sometimes think, in fact, that the closer one gets to sentimentality without actually giving in to it, the better. Or to put that in terms more in tune with what I have been arguing, it is a great accomplishment in a poem to take content that is very close to a common emotional experience that can easily be sentimentalized but render it with a depth of feeling and attention to the particular that is entirely unsentimental.

I can immediately think of two great poems that do just that. The first is Robert Hayden's classic "Those Winter Sundays," a portrait of an emotionally distant father, which begins with an account of the hard-working and temperamental father rising every day, even on Sunday, to warm the house by building back up the previous night's fire.[13]

This poem could easily have focused on the coziness of the fire, or painted an unmixed and all-admiring portrait of the father. Alternately, it could have railed like a cardboard Sylvia Plath against the evils of patriarchy. But instead, Hayden took the tougher road of telling us about *his* particular father and their relationship, and as he looks back he sees harshness but also love in his boyhood home. In that particularity there is a power to impart universal truth about the complexity of family relationships, something no sentimental poem can achieve.

The other poem that springs to mind is Gerard Manley Hopkins's "Spring and Fall." The images are fresh and striking in their particularity:

> Márgarét, áre you gríeving
> Over Goldengrove unleaving?
> Leáves like the things of man, you
> With your fresh thoughts care for, can you?
> Ah! ás the heart grows older
> It will come to such sights colder
> By and by, nor spare a sigh

---

12. Kooser, *Poetry Home Repair*, 56–59.
13. Hayden, "Those Winter Sundays," in *Collected Poems*, 41.

> Though worlds of wanwood leafmeal lie;
> And yet you wíll weep and know why.
> Now no matter, child, the name:
> Sórrow's spríngs áre the same.
> Nor mouth had, no nor mind, expressed
> What heart heard of, ghost guessed:
> It ís the blight man was born for,
> It is Margaret you mourn for.[14]

The poem places its sense of loss into particular images of "Goldengrove unleaving" and "worlds of wanwood" that "leafmeal lie." Through these images, Hopkins tackles tricky subjects, subjects that could easily lure one into sentimentality, such as the passing of time and the value and loss of innocence. The poet, however, avoids sentimentality by keeping the poem grounded in the particular, emphasizing real vegetation and a real child, the Margaret, of the first and last lines. The poem is an excellent example of a poet engaging with strong emotion and age-old truths, of a poet risking sentimentality, without giving in to the sentimental impulse.

Once the Christian reader has dined on poetic fare as rich as this, how could he or she be satisfied with the thin gruel of sentimentality or with the hard biscuit of the cynical? Once we have known the sacred touch of real love, two made one flesh, both gift from God and image of God's love for us, how could we ever again be content with poetic pornography?

---

14. Hopkins, "Spring and Fall," in *Major Works*, 152.

4

Writing the Fallen World

Not the Golden World

THE ENGLISH RENAISSANCE POET and courtier Sir Philip Sidney famously states in his *The Defense of Poesy,* "Nature never set forth the earth in so rich tapestry as divers poets have done; neither with pleasant rivers, fruitful trees, sweet-smelling flowers, nor whatsoever else may make the too-much-loved earth more lovely; her world is brazen, the poets only deliver a golden."[1] I hesitate to begin the chapter by picking a quarrel with such an august person as Sidney, but I don't think good poetry presents "the golden world" at all. With the term *golden*, of course, Sidney means to evoke the classical idea of the ages of the world, as in the Greek poet Hesiod's account of the decline of the world from the first age of gold down through three more until the fifth and current age of iron. This myth, also found in Ovid's *Metamorphoses,* was often evoked in the Renaissance as an allegory for the fall of man, with the golden world as an image of Eden. When we understand this background, we can see that Sidney is suggesting that poets present an unfallen world in their poetry. Of course, some poets try to do just that, but most don't. Those who do generally write boring poetry.

Perhaps it is best to let another writer of stature contend with Sidney. What Flannery O'Connor has to say about novels applies as well to poetry:

---

1. Sidney, *Major Works,* 216.

> The serious writer has always taken the flaw in human nature as his starting point, usually the flaw in an otherwise admirable character. Drama usually bases itself on the bedrock of original sin, whether the writer thinks in theological terms or not. Then, too, any character in a serious novel is supposed to carry a burden of meaning larger than himself. The novelist doesn't write about people in a vacuum; he writes about people in a world where something is obviously lacking, where there is the general mystery of incompleteness and the particular tragedy of our own times to be demonstrated, and the novelist tries to give you, within the form of the book, a total experience of human nature at any time.[2]

Contrary to the Christian writer who thinks it somehow more pious to present the perfect world, O'Connor speaks of the writer's obligation to faithfully depict the sense of something lacking in the fallen world. She notes that the sense of "drama," of tension and import, in a work of literature depends on telling about fallen people in a fallen world. If at times it seems that all poems are a version of *Paradise Lost*, that is partly due to the talent and influence of Milton but partly due to there being no other truly compelling human story other than our fall and redemption.

Thus while the poet engages with the goodness of creation, he or she must also engage with the something that is obviously missing, to put it in O'Connor's terms. As we saw in the last chapter, that means avoiding sentimentality. Writing truthfully about the fallen world, however, is more than a negative practice, more than a matter of what we don't do. It is also a matter of engaging even with joy within the context of the fallen world. As artists and as evaluators of art, we should always remember where we are.

In his *Confessions*, Augustine raises the interesting possibility that all our happiness is the product of our dim, inherited memory of Eden. He points out that even the unhappy must, in some sense, possess happiness, or else they would not know what they are missing, would not know that they are unhappy. This thought sends him into speculation: "My inquiry is whether this knowing is in the memory because, if it is there, we had happiness once. I do not now ask whether we were all happy individually or only corporately in that man who first sinned, in whom we all died and from whom we were all born into a condition of misery. My question is whether the happy life is in the memory. For we would not love it if we did no know what it is."[3] Despite his demur about not now raising the question,

---

2. O'Connor, *Mystery and Manners*, 167.
3. Augustine, *Confessions*, 196–97.

Augustine does indeed pose a poignant possibility in tracing our very capacity for both happiness—and, by logical inverse, unhappiness—to some distant recollection of humanity in an unfallen state. The idea has powerful implications for the way we think about poetry's ability to depict both joy and sorrow.

The In-Between

For poetry to resonate with a distant memory of Eden, it must reject the gnostic view of creation as inherently evil on the one hand and the romantic view of nature as an unfallen perfection on the other. From the Christian standpoint, art has an aesthetic responsibility to reality. It must capture the *in-betweeness*, the something good and the "something missing," of our lives in the fallen world. It has always seemed to me that Shakespeare's "tragicomedies," especially *The Winter's Tale*, capture the Christian vision of life far better than his comedies or even his great tragedies.

W. H. Auden captures something of this *in-betweeness* in his great poem, "As I Walked Out One Evening," which I urge all Christians to read. Early in the poem we hear the exaggerated declarations of young love, culminating in the declaration that the lovers' union returns them to Edenic paradise. We all, of course, yearn for the purity and perfection of the world's first love, a time before sin spoiled all. It is easy to give ourselves to fantasies of Eden returned before the ripeness of time, and it becomes apparent that the personification the poem calls "Time" represents the human experience of life in a fallen world. Indeed, in one sense, "time" is a good name for the in-between, the time after the fall and before the final redemption. Auden sums up fallen experience very succinctly in several stanzas that detail the tedious minutiae of fallen existence, the little things that eat away at us. We live, the poet comes to assert, in a world of bother and anxiety. Auden's powerful images of winter ravaging a pastoral landscape evoke the equally powerful images of the Twenty-third Psalm, reminding us that "the valley of the shadow of death" is not a bad neighborhood in ancient Israel but rather a succinct summation of this life, a life that is a full of "green pastures" but also constantly under the shadow of the penalty for sin. No matter how lovely the dancer or how talented the young athlete, time has its way.

Auden, however, doesn't leave it there. In the poem's final stanzas, he captures perfectly that sense of *in-betweeness* that acknowledges also the good of creation and the promise of redemption as he calls on the reader to love his fellow fallen man despite all our flaws. Rather than replace the naïve lover's exclamations with easy cynicism and cheap snark, Auden offers a deeper view of love, a view of what it means to love in the fallen world. There is a certain amount of frisson in the picture, a feeling of "someday but not yet." This view of life is sober yet hopeful. It dismisses neither pain nor love. It is true in its depiction of human experience and thus resonates with the reader as real art.

One imagines that if Auden had included only the naïve, early stanzas of the poem, if it had ended triumphantly with the lovers returned to Eden, the poem may have been instantly popular with superficial readers but would have faded as quickly as a top forty love song. Happy poems need some sense of the fall, no matter how muted. Of course, it is hard to find a poem with no sense of fallenness, even in an age like ours in which our comforts and achievements might push the fallen nature of the world to the back of even the Christian mind. But poems lose aesthetic power inasmuch as they attempt to push fallenness out of the poem, inasmuch as they try to give us a "Golden World" without complication. When this attempt is combined with a certain preciousness, the result is the sentimentality we examined in the last chapter. A poem, however, can avoid sentimentality but still fail to engage meaningfully with fallenness.

For example, were A. E. Houseman to have written only this first stanza of one of his most famous poems, it is doubtful the poem would have proved so enduring:

> Loveliest of trees, the cherry now
> Is hung with bloom along the bough,
> And stands about the woodland ride
> Wearing white for Eastertide.

Thus far the poem is indeed *lovely*. It is musical and vivid. It is the next stanza, however, with its acknowledgment of the fallenness of our world, that carries the poem over from mere loveliness into real beauty:

> Now, of my threescore years and ten,
> Twenty will not come again,
> And take from seventy springs a score,
> It only leaves me fifty more.

Now we feel the passing of time that calls us to savor all the more the loveliness of the blossoming trees. To mere prettiness has been added poignancy. Housman's evocation of beauty and transience in the cherry blossom is reminiscent of the Japanese aesthetic of *wabi-sabi*, the principle that impermanence and age add a subtle but powerful beauty to nature and human life. Houseman doesn't end the poem bleakly, however. His final stanza shows a determination for beauty:

> And since to look at things in bloom
> Fifty springs are little room,
> About the woodlands I will go
> To see the cherry hung with snow.[4]

A small masterpiece, Houseman's poem manages to be prettily scenic while speaking an undeniable truth of human life without a hint of sentimentality. It accomplishes this by acknowledging the reality of the fall even while expressing a deep appreciation for the natural world.

A poem might even be excellent in several other ways but, lacking a sense of the world's imperfection, it can still lack the friction necessary for good art. Perhaps contemporary Americans, with our comfortable lives and escapist tendencies, are in particular danger of forgetting the fall, until we are personally faced with suffering, tragedy, or travail.

Bad Words

One element of the literature of the fallen world that Christian readers are often uncomfortable with is fallen people's tendency to use very fallen diction. In other words, what ought we to think of "bad language" in poetry? Should the Christian poet avoid all potentially offensive language? Is recourse to "swear words" a sure sign of a weak vocabulary, as so many of our mothers told us?

Perhaps the most relevant Scripture to this question is Ephesians 4:29, with its injunction to "Let no corrupting talk come out of your mouths, but only such as is good for building up, as fits the occasion, that it may give grace to those who hear." It would be a travesty of biblical interpretation, however, to limit the definition of "corrupting talk" to the level of diction, as if God didn't care *what* we said only *how* we said it.

To take one provocative example, the word *shit* is considered "corrupt" by most Christian readers, but it is a "bad word" only due to the accidents of history. After the French-speaking Normans conquered England

---

4. Houseman, II, in *The Collected Poems*, 11.

and exterminated much of the old English aristocracy, it was considered "rude" or "vulgar"—the original sense of the first term being "like the peasantry" and of the second being "using the language of the locals"—to refer to things by their Anglo-Saxon term. But does God really care if we use the French-rooted "poop" or, better yet, the Latinate "defecate," rather than the Anglo-Saxon term? I seriously doubt it.

What God does care about is the aim of our language. Paul clearly defines "corrupting talk" in opposition to the kind of communication that edifies and ministers grace. I've heard several instances of "bless your heart" and "I'll pray for you" that, given the tone and intent of the comment, could qualify as corrupt.

But why would a Christian writer use "off-color" language, and why should a Christian reader countenance it? The first reason is accuracy. When the poet looks to represent the speech of others, it should be done accurately in a way that doesn't diminish the friction of the fallen world. A poet shouldn't smooth things over, shouldn't try to give us a "golden world" in which dock hands or fraternity boys talk like Sunday school teachers. Our first model should be the Holy Scripture, which never sugarcoats reality.

The Christian poet should, of course, avoid committing blasphemy, which does not mean that one should not write about the blasphemy of characters. If one wishes to learn how to report on blasphemy without committing it, Dante models just that in his depiction of Capaneus in *Inferno*, canto fourteen. In describing this rebel against God, Dante alludes to but does not directly quote whatever the sinner says against his maker. Much can be said for knowing when to quote, when to paraphrase, and when merely to gesture toward another person's words and actions.

The Christian poet should also be careful never to use language in such a way as to diminish the dignity of human beings made in the image of God. "Vulgar" or "off-color" language often has this aim, and, while it may have a place in the reported speech of characters—the bad words of bad people—the poet should be careful to distance it from the poem's dominant viewpoint. It is usually immediately apparent when the main aim of language is to demean someone. That much is fairly obvious. Dehumanizing language comes in all kinds of varieties, however, some four letter and some not. As Hamlet reminds us, "one can smile and smile and be a villain." If we limit our concern about dehumanizing language to four-letter words, we have addressed the issue in only the most infantile way.

Despite all this, there are times when a poem can achieve even a greater spiritual forcefulness through the use of language we normally consider impolite. One of the best descriptions I have read of baptism is in a poem by the late Franz Wright, "Baptism," in which he says, "That insane asshole is dead / I drowned him / and he's not coming back."[5] I would contend that the word *asshole* adds spiritual punch to the poem. It conveys far better than could "jerk" or "bad guy" the dramatic change in the poet's life. Through the vulgar language, the reader is pushed to take baptism very seriously and to look at it with fresh eyes. The language is consonant with the force of experience in the fallen world. That said, if asked to read a poem during our worship service, I will most likely not choose Wright's poem but rather something by Donne, Herbert, or Jane Kenyon. "'All things are lawful,' but not all things are helpful. 'All things are lawful,' but not all things build up" (1 Corinthians 10:23). There's no sense in scandalizing the Sunday school teachers.

I have never hesitated, however, to teach to college-age students poems that use "salty language," even at the Christian college where I teach now. I am careful, of course, to show why the language is appropriate to the poem. Take for instance Christian Wiman's poem "Five Houses Down," from his magnificent book, *Every Riven Thing*. The poem paints a loving portrait of a rough-edged, bachelor junkman who lived down the street when the narrator was a young man. It is a humane and compassionate depiction of a person on the margins of respectable society. Such people do not use the language of the Sunday school lesson or the PTA meeting, and to depict the character truly, and thus lovingly, he must be made to speak the way any grown person knows this character would speak. Wiman is, however, himself alert to the complexities of language. Curiously, the poet tells us

> His barklike earthquake curses
> were not curses, for he could *goddamn*
> a slipped wrench and *shitfuck* a stuck latch,
> but one bad word from me
> made his whole being
> twang like a nail mis-struck. *Ain't no call for that,
> Son, no call at all.*[6]

---

5. Wright, "Baptism," in *Walking to Martha's Vineyard*, 44.
6. Wiman, "Five Houses Down," in *Every Riven Thing*, 8.

The language is shocking and is meant to be. In his own profanity and vulgarity the character's fallen humanity is clear, but in his concern for the young narrator's purity we see, too, his redeemable humanity, the *imago Dei*. It is a strikingly honest depiction and a powerful example of the in-betweeness of fallen life. I doubt Wiman could have painted the portrait so compellingly by dancing around the junkman's vocabulary. I'm not sure this poem would be as authentically Christian without the "objectionable" language.

The Minor Theme

In *Art and the Bible*, Francis Schaeffer speaks of Christianity's "major theme" and "minor theme." Schaeffer defines the major theme as "the meaningfulness and purposefulness of life" and the minor theme as "the abnormality of the revolting world."[7] He then explains that "[i]f our Christian art only emphasizes the major theme, then it is not fully Christian but simply romantic art. And let us say with sorrow that for years our Sunday school literature has been romantic in its art and has had very little to do with genuine Christian art. Older Christians may wonder what is wrong with this art and wonder why their kids are turned off by it, but the answer is simple. It's romantic. It's based on the notion that Christianity has only an optimistic note."[8] Schaeffer adds that it is possible to overly focus on the minor theme and forget the major, and of course that happens. We can easily fall into loving the shadow itself and forgetting that we were only looking at it as a reminder of the reality of the sun. But Christian art today is in greater danger of forgetting the doctrine of the fall than it is of forgetting the doctrine of redemption. Christian art more usually fails by presenting itself as if *Ecclesiastes* weren't also as much a part of Holy Scripture as our favorite verses in the fifteenth chapter of 1 Corinthians. But how can we celebrate redemption if we don't need redemption, or how can we credit the Holy Spirit with our sanctification if we seem to think that, once we are redeemed we need no sanctification?

Christian art can do better than that. Ideally, as in the plays of Shakespeare, the major theme and the minor theme reinforce each other, our eventual arrival in the new heaven and new earth made all the sweeter by our time in-between. No work of art that ignores that in-betweeness can

---

7. Schaeffer, *Art and the Bible*, 83–84.
8. Schaeffer, *Art and the Bible*, 86.

A Poetics of Orthodoxy

every really resonate with us. It will seem a lie not because it is "happy" but rather because it is merely happy. As much as we might want to push the doctrine into the background, our experiences tell us that we live in a fallen world. The poems that really touch us are the poems that acknowledge this reality.

5

The Gift of Beauty

Disruptive Beauty

B. H. Fairchild's long, fugue-like poem, "Beauty," is surely one of the best poems of the last fifty years. Weaving together memories of his childhood among the resilient residents of the southern plains—particularly a strange occurrence of exhibitionism in his father's machine shop—with a trip he took much later in life with his wife to Florence, Fairchild prompts us to ponder what we talk about when we talk about "beauty." At the heart of the poem is the observation that beauty is often somehow embarrassing. "[N]o male member of my family has ever used / this word in my hearing or anyone else's except / in reference, perhaps, to a new pickup or dead deer," he wryly observes.[1] Beauty is disconcerting for men "who knew the true meaning of labor and money and other / hard, true things and did not, did not ever, use the word, *beauty*."[2] Beauty makes strong men afraid.

What is it that is embarrassing about beauty? Why does it provoke in strong men the need to be stronger, the fear of weakness? It must be that beauty makes us somehow aware of our own limitation, of something small in us. In Rainer Maria Rilke's great poem "Archaic Torso of Apollo," the reader is carried along on an encounter with beauty that ends with the sudden, famous insistence that "you must change your life." Nothing in

---

1. Fairchild, "Beauty," in *Blue Buick*, 61.
2. Fairchild, "Beauty," in *Blue Buick*, 63.

the poem suggests that the change is what we would normally call a moral change. Rather, it seems to have something to do with recognizing the way real beauty inevitably casts judgement on our mundane indifference to it. Beauty calls our priorities into question.

This disturbing quality of beauty is what Fairchild gestures toward in his story of two young men who disrobe in the middle of the machine shop. He tells us not only of the nearly violent reaction of the other men in the shop but also of his own sudden memory of the men many years later as he stands looking at Donatello's graceful, stunning statue of David. Beauty is disruptive. In this, and other ways, it is like grace.

When, as in previous chapters, I denounce sentimentality and emphasize the importance of artistic engagement with the world's fallenness, I am often accused of preferring ugliness to beauty. Nothing could be further from the truth. As I tried to make clear in chapter 3, sentimentality is not the friend of true beauty but rather its enemy. Furthermore, the sentimental rears its ugly head just as often these days in attempts at "grittiness" or even dehumanizing brutality (I am thinking here of the aesthetic of artists like the filmmaker Quentin Tarantino, which is, on the whole, ugly, deadening, and thoroughly sentimental).

When one writes the fallen world, one is not attempting to occlude the transcendental beauty of God's perfect creation and plan. Rather, the serious artist attempts to know this transcendental perfection in practically the only way we can from this vantage point, by our distance from it. We know beauty like a distant mountain peak, and we are sometimes forced to measure its height by the length of the shadow it casts between itself and us.

In his powerful sonnet "God's Grandeur" Gerard Manley Hopkins acknowledges the fall when he notes that the whole world "wears man's smudge and shares man's smell," yet he asserts that, even so, "There lives the dearest freshness deep down things[.]"[3] Even though we live in a fallen world, we can still see the beauty of God's creation. As C. S. Lewis famously says, "If I find in myself a desire which no experience in this world can satisfy, the most probable explanation is that I was made for another world."[4] To reject sentimentality and to write from within the fallen world is not to reject beauty. Rather, it is to take beauty seriously. A counterfeit artist may attempt to pass around a cheap beauty, just as Dietrich Bonhoeffer warned us that counterfeit Christianity will attempt to pass around "cheap grace,"

---

3. Hopkins, "God's Grandeur," in *Major Works*, 128.
4. Lewis, *The Complete C. S. Lewis*, 76.

but neither of the false versions comes close to the real thing. Neither cheap beauty nor cheap grace are, as are the authentic versions, the signature of God.

The Testimony of Beauty

Many modern patterns of thought conspire against beauty. The soft utilitarianism that saturates our society tells us that beauty is just a distraction from the really useful things. Given postmodernism's tendency to reduce all aspects of human life to the struggle for power, the proponents of "social justice" and "the hermeneutics of suspicion" are apt to see any talk of beauty as merely a means of covering up some injustice. Influencing all these positions is the postmodern relativism that says all beauty is just in the mind of the beholder.

Unfortunately, even the church often conspires against beauty, as certain forms of Protestantism treat beauty with the suspicion that it is simply a trapdoor into idolatry. We think we are somehow guarded against the idols in our heart by surrounding ourselves with as drab and dreary an environment as possible. My fellow Protestants all too often see beauty as the province, and the downfall, of the Catholic church alone.

To put it plainly, whether one rejects it as a medieval Catholic relic or as just plain useless, beauty is not modern enough for many people. And yet, as Francis Schaeffer points out, in *Art and the Bible*, God cares about beauty. Schaeffer sees the Lord's instructions for the decoration of the temple as irrefutable evidence of God's cherishing of the beautiful.[5] The Lord calls for the best craftsmen and the best materials in order to make a temple that is not only functional but also aesthetically pleasing. The instructions for the temple seem to make a point of calling out for what is certainly well beyond the pale of necessity.

Although rational, theological exposition of beauty has a long and fruitful history in Western thought, which we will explore below, most of us first encounter beauty's relationship to God not *in* an argument but rather *as* an argument. As we will see, mankind's constant intuition about beauty has been that beauty points beyond itself to the divine. The twentieth-century Catholic philosopher Dietrich von Hildebrand saw in beauty a form of God's self-expression, at once both innately valuable and indispensable for human flourishing:

---

5. Schaeffer, *Art and the Bible*, 26.

> Above all, beauty is a reflection of God, a reflection of His own infinite beauty, a genuine value, something that is important-in-itself, something that praises God. This means that the question of the contribution that beauty makes to human life is secondary. Nevertheless, this question is highly significant, since it is extremely important to understand the central objective good that the existence of beautiful things is for the human person. And from the perspective of the ecology of the spirit, it is necessary for us to grasp that the elimination of poetry from life, the destruction of the beauty of nature and especially of the beauty of architecture, terribly impoverishes human existence, and indeed damages and undermines it.[6]

We need beauty to be well because beauty is a major form of God's presence. As David Bentley Hart argues, this is why the Bible and Christian tradition speak of our incarnated Lord as supremely beautiful.[7]

I was blessed in college with many long, late-night conversations in the dorms, another rite of youth I sometimes fear has been endangered by the proliferation of electronic distractions. Many of these conversations, naturally, were about God and how we can know God exists. On one night I vividly remember, a good friend, usually a far more pious and orthodox Christian than was I at the time, was expressing a deep and anguished doubt of God's existence. Such resources of traditional apologetics as I had were completely inadequate for reassuring my friend, as he was not suffering from an intellectual misgiving but rather from a lack of feeling God's presence. Finally, my feeble intellect exhausted, I took my friend by the arm and tugged him from the room, down the hall, and out into the parking lot, where a full moon glowed voluminously over the parked cars and the leafy tops of the surrounding trees. "Look," was the only argument I had.

It was enough. My friend, in tears and in prayer, acknowledged anew the reality of God's nearness to us. Though the dramatic nature of this scene is due, no doubt, largely to youthful romanticism, the core of the experience has been repeated throughout human history. Beauty inevitably carries with it the sense that God is near.

Many years after that night in the dorms, I went through my own period of doubt, often struggling with my faith on the long, solitary drive to work. Ultimately, I found my faith restored in drawing near to our Lord in prayer and in reading the Scripture, but the way back to these good things

---

6. Hildebrand, *Aesthetics*, 2–3.
7. Hart, *Beauty of the Infinite*.

seems to have been opened to me as I sat in the office parking lot and gazed at a particular tree, reddened and luminous in its October glory. I could think of scientific, materialist reasons for the tree to turn red. I could not explain, however, how it should be that the *beauty* of the tree should so powerfully affect me, why it should call so to my soul. Why should it matter so much to me that the tree is red? What language is this that my soul instinctively knows? The mystery of beauty points us to the deeper mystery of being. Looking at that tree, I knew that beauty is the voice of God and that the voice of God is the presence of God.

Contrary to the modern tendency to be indifferent to beauty, the great early Christian philosopher Augustine of Hippo struggled with guilt over his great susceptibility to beauty, recognizing how loving it more than God can lead us astray even while God is himself ultimate beauty. Augustine was, of course, right to be wary of falling into idolatry. Yet, in some sense, in the young Augustine's powerful attraction to poetry, theater, and female charm, we can see dim hints of the desire that will draw him to God, who is the ultimate Beauty and thus the source of all that we call beautiful. Looking back on his life, Augustine says to God,

> Late have I loved you, beauty so old and so new: late have I loved you. And see, you were within and I was in the external world and sought you there, and in my unlovely state I plunged into those lovely created things which you made. You were with me, and I was not with you. The lovely things kept me far from you, though if they did not have their existence in you, they had no existence at all. You called and cried out loud and shattered my deafness. You were radiant and resplendent, you put to flight my blindness. You were fragrant, and I drew in my breath and now pant after you. I tasted you, and I feel but hunger and thirst for you. You touched me, and I am set on fire to attain the peace which is yours.[8]

The young Augustine was no more wrong to seek beauty than he was to seek truth and goodness, but, like many of us, he failed for far too long to look through beauty to the ultimate beauty of God. He failed, for much too long, to see beauty as a language that speaks of something beyond itself. Yet, one can imagine how much worse off he would have been had he instead been utterly insensitive to all beauty. He might have avoided false gods at the price of having missed the one true God. If God was calling out to him

---

8. Augustine, *Confessions*, 201.

through the beauty of creation, then Augustine's perception of beauty was a blessing, a path home provided by God himself.

Although much has been made of Augustine's regret for his susceptibility to beauty, we should also note the high value he places on it. Even though he roots his thought in Platonism, along with Scripture, Augustine is no gnostic, having rejected the Manicheanism of his youth. For Augustine, the beauty of the things of this world is not a dead end. Indeed the error he regrets was in treating beauty as a stopping point, failing to hear the voice of God in beautiful things. No simple-minded ascetic, Augustine sees beauty as a form of testimony to the existence and nature of God.

I sometimes think that atheism, rather than an intellectual block, is a form of tone-deafness. After all, it cannot be just an intellectual defect, since there are so many atheists of great intelligence, so many brilliant and prominent scholars and thinkers who fail to hear the song creation sings about its Maker. I think the failure to believe is a failure to heed God's voice in the conscience but also perhaps a failure to hear God's voice with the aesthetic faculties.

A few pages earlier in *Confessions*, Augustine says something similar:

> Surely this beauty should be self-evident to all who are of sound mind. Then why does it not speak to everyone in the same way? Animals both small and large see it, but they cannot put a question about it. In them reason does not sit in judgement upon the deliverances of the senses. But human beings can put a question so that "the invisible things of God are understood and seen through the things which are made" (Rom. 1:20). Yet by love of created things they are subdued by them, and being thus made subject become incapable of exercising judgement. Moreover, created things do not answer those who question them if power to judge is lost. There is no alteration in the voice which is their beauty. If one person sees while another sees and questions, it is not that they appear one way to the first and another way to the second. It is rather that the created order speaks to all but is understood by those who hear its outward voice and compare it with the truth within themselves.[9]

We can fail to hear the voice that is beauty, thinking, like the young Augustine before his conversion, that beautiful things speak only for and of themselves. When we do so, we fail to ask the important question, "What does beauty say to us about the nature of reality, about the truth beneath

---

9. Augustine, *Confessions*, 184.

the surface of appearances?" We can look at the full moon and see only a chunk of rock in orbit, never asking ourselves why we are compelled to keep looking.

What Augustine calls "the question" that beauty provokes has been taken very seriously by the Christian intellectual tradition, beginning even before Augustine's time. Brendan Thomas Sammon has traced how the theological approach to beauty begins, like so much in Western culture, in the synthesis of the Judeo-Christian worldview with Greco-Roman thought.[10] Sammon points out that, in the Old Testament, "beauty is deeply and profoundly bound up with God's very being; simply put, God is beauty itself."[11]

In the early church, this understanding of the beautiful God who says "I am" is augmented by the Greek exploration of being, or *ousia*, primarily through the Platonic tradition. There certainly is no one Christian understanding of beauty.[12] It is safe to say, however, that, in general, Christian thought associates beauty with God's ultimate *being*. James Matthew Wilson sums up this tradition as it is manifested in the work of Jacques Maritain: "If form is the principle of being of any and every thing, and if it is form that constitutes beauty, then beauty must be convertible with being: every thing, insofar as it has being, must have to that extent beauty. Along with unity, goodness, and truth, beauty must be one of the transcendental properties of being—and, as God is being Itself, so these properties must name God."[13] For the Christian, then, beauty is something more than mere *pleasantness* or even *loveliness*. It is a way in which the infinite God makes Himself known to us.

In his book *The Beauty of the Infinite*, David Bentley Hart explains how the Christian understanding of beauty stands counter to both pagan and modern/postmodern forms of nihilism that would leave the infinite at an un-crossable distance from us. In a gratuity born out of the loving nature of the Trinity, God comes to us in beauty: "God's gracious action in creation belongs from the first to that delight, pleasure, and regard that the Trinity enjoys from eternity, as an outward and unnecessary expression of that love; and thus creation must be received before all else as gift and

---

10. Sammon, *Called to Attraction*.
11. Sammon, *Called to Attraction*, 16.
12. For a sense of the complexity see, in addition to Sammon, Eco, *Art and Beauty*.
13. Wilson, *Vision of the Soul*, 194.

beauty."[14] Beauty is a picture of grace, grace's very mirror. It comes unasked for and undeserved to lift us out of ourselves and above our petty concerns. It is, however, also like grace in that it can be resisted. We can harden our hearts to it. One thing good poetry can do is teach us to respond to beauty.

The Pursuit of Beauty

Our response to beauty seems often to take the form of longing. This is why beauty is often experienced as a kind of pang. An encounter with beauty stirs in us the knowledge of something beyond, or behind, material reality, but not wholly antagonistic to that reality. Drawing on the writings of Gregory of Nyssa, David Bentley Hart describes the soul drawn to beauty as "drawn on forever by a desire enkindled always anew by the beauty that lies beyond the beauty already possessed, receiving the visible as an image of God's transcendent loveliness, but longing all the more to enjoy that beauty face-to-face, the soul experiences ceaseless delight precisely in that its desire can know no final satiety[.]"[15] A true encounter with beauty is an experience of delectable longing, of precious pain. We can call it a form of *eros*.

Like metaphor, beauty points us toward the meaningfulness of things, but beauty does so though the experience of longing. Again in Hart, we find this summation:

> It is the pleasingness of the other's otherness, the goodness that God sees in creation, that wakes desire to what it must affirm and what it must not violate, and shows love the measure of charitable detachment that must temper its elations; it is only in desire that the beautiful is known and its invitation heard. Here Christian thought learns something, perhaps, of how the Trinitarian love of God—and the love God requires of creatures—is eros and agape at once: a desire for the other that delights in the distance of otherness. But desire must also be cultivated; the beautiful does not always immediately commend itself to every taste; Christ's beauty, like that of Isaiah's suffering servant, is not expressed in vacuous comeliness or shadowless glamor, but calls for a love that is charitable, that is not dismayed by distance or mystery, and that can

---

14. Hart, *Beauty of the Infinite*, 249.
15. Hart, *Beauty of the Infinite*, 195.

repent of its failure to see; this is to acquire what Augustine calls a taste for the beauty of God[.][16]

This acquisition of taste has, historically and until very recently, been at the heart of everything called "education" in the Western world. It was assumed that the job of the teacher was to instruct the pupil in love for the thing worthy of love, to shape the desire of the young for the pursuit of the true, the good, and the beautiful. This process takes time, which is why it is tragic to see education from preschool through college abandoning the arts to focus on more "practical" subjects.

Cultivating our sensitivity to beauty, a cultivation of proper desire, is why we read, beyond the simple, utilitarian motive of acquiring information. Drawing on Augustine, James K. A. Smith has consistently argued that "we are what we love."[17] He means that we are shaped by the things toward which we orient our desire, which is why we should be careful to aim ourselves at God. Beauty teaches us to love what is loveable and, through that, to love God. "Our culture," as James Matthew Wilson says, "lies to itself in denying the reality of beauty, and barbarizes and narrows its intellect in treating aesthetic education as unimportant to the formation of a complex human being."[18] When we let the aesthetic sense die in us, when we lose the longing, we fail to live up to the charge given us in Philippians 4:8. Moreover, we miss the life abundant that Jesus himself offers to us (John 10: 10).

One of the most powerful expressions of the longing evoked by beauty I know of is W. B. Yeats's "The Song of Wandering Aengus." Although Yeats apparently wrote the poem out of a frustrated, unrequited love for the Irish beauty and revolutionary, Maude Gonne, it speaks far more universally of the way beauty tugs us toward a deeper world and our ultimate home. He begins with "I went out to the hazel wood, / Because a fire was in my head," a succinct and exquisite expression of innate human restlessness.[19] One thinks of Augustine's famous opening line in his confession to God, "our heart is restless until it rests in you."[20] Having done what men throughout time have done when at a loss for any other meaningful action, gone fishing, the narrator of the poem returns to his cabin with his catch. Soon, however, he discovers that the "little silver trout" he caught has been transformed

16. Hart, *Beauty of the Infinite*, 20.
17. Smith, *What You Love* and *Desiring the Kingdom*.
18. Wilson, *Vision of the Soul*, 231.
19. Yeats, "The Song of Wandering Aengus," in *Collected Works*, 59.
20. Augustine, *Confessions*, 3.

into "a glimmering girl / With apple blossom in her hair[.]"[21] When he created this image, Yeats was thinking of the first time he saw Maude Gonne, framed by the window behind her, through which he could see the apple blossoms, but the image suggests more generally a beauty suspended between heaven and earth.

The moment is fleeting, however, as the fairy girl calls his name just before she "ran / and faded through the brightening air."[22] In allegorical form, this is a moment anyone who has ever had his "name called" by beauty will recognize. The soul is called by beauty even as it somehow remains out of reach. Beauty always calls our name and runs. This is the experience outlined by Plato's Socrates in *The Symposium*, an early recognition of beauty's deeper form of *eros*.

Having given a succinct picture of the sort of encounter with beauty that demands one change one's life, Yeats's poem culminates in a passionate declaration of longing and dedication:

> Though I am old with wandering
> Through hollow lands and hilly lands,
> I will find out where she has gone,
> And kiss her lips and take her hands,
> And walk among long dappled grass,
> And pluck till time and times are done
> The silver apples of the moon,
> The golden apples of the sun.[23]

As Gregory of Nyssa insisted, those who pursue beauty resign themselves to the perpetuity of that pursuit, confident in its attainment only in the beyond, represented in Yeats's poem by the ethereal images of the silver and golden apples of the heavenly bodies. One completes this poem not with a sense of frustration at unrequited love but rather with the impression that the endless pursuit of beauty is the most noble mode of human life. Beauty is a necessary disruption.

That we perpetually seek beauty does not mean we should ever fear exhausting it. Because it has its source in the infinite God, beauty is inexhaustible. This insight should relieve the contemporary artist of the heavy burden that is our sense of belatedness. Beauty has not been exhausted. It

---

21. Yeats, "The Song of Wandering Aengus," in *Collected Works*, 59–60.
22. Yeats, "The Song of Wandering Aengus," in *Collected Works*, 60.
23. Yeats, "The Song of Wandering Aengus," in *Collected Works*, 60.

was not finished off by the romantic poets or finally consumed by Rossetti or Tennyson. Beauty has a place in the modern world. Because the source of all beauty is the limitless, infinite God, beauty is still and always possible. We don't need to settle for kitsch or sentimentality or pure irony or unadulterated rage. We don't need to settle for the merely clever or the snarky. We don't need to settle for the simply pleasant or smugly confirming. Beauty is still possible. It can still inspire and trouble us. The artist's job is to pursue it.

The Particularity of Beauty

I've gone so far afield in this chapter only to emphasize that any orthodox Christian approach to poetry must acknowledge the central place of beauty in artistic pursuits. But what does beauty look like in poem form? We know God's infinite beauty only as it is manifested in creation. Brendan Thomas Sammon argues that theology, in a line from Francis of Assisi to Søren Kierkegaard, discovers the importance of beauty's particularity in the particularity of Christ's incarnation: "Perhaps the single most important contribution to a theology of beauty that Francis made was a return to the particular individuality of Jesus. In the Incarnation, God had entered completely into the particularities of human life. It was an event that inspired the gathering of a community not only of practice but also of thoughtful reflection."[24] Thomas Aquinas emphasizes that "[a]ll things come from God's beauty, which is a fullness of intelligible content, and all things share in that fullness in their own unique way. Their beauty is their communication of this unique share in the divine fullness. This is a fullness that can only appear in time and space through that thing's unique form as a particular 'this.'"[25] This would seem to be the thought behind Gerard Manley Hopkins's concept of *inscape*, his word for the unique created nature of each thing, every thing's *thisness*. We are thus returned to chapter 1 and our discussion of the poetic image.

Poetry will not achieve beauty without concrete images of particular things. This is so because each thing has its being, and thus its beauty, in light of God's ultimate being, meaning that God's beauty shines in his creation. In other words, things don't reflect their maker by becoming less themselves but rather by becoming more themselves. The more that *becoming* approaches *being* the more we call it *beauty*. Precisely because things

---

24. Sammon, *Called to Attraction*, 78.
25. Sammon, *Called to Attraction*, 101–2.

are only because of God, their being and their goodness are synonymous with their beauty. The artist who seeks to capture beauty must first attend to what *is*.

What does that look like in poetry? Of course, it is hard to give examples of beauty not because it is scarce but rather because it is so abundant, being wrapped up with the abundance of God's creation. We define beauty by pointing to it, by sharing it, perhaps in the same way that forgiveness is the proper response to forgiveness. So, I can only say that, for instance, Yeats's "Song of Wandering Aengus" and the opening lines of Ezra Pound's *Cantos* continue to haunt me, or that Theodore Roethke's lines describing a snail in his poem "Lost Son" struck me as beautiful the first time I read them. The whole of Frost's "Birches" seems to me a supreme beauty equaled only by medieval masters such as Dante. Clearly, the beauty of these lines is related to the images, the sounds, the form, and the feeling. But the total is more than the sum of the parts. Nonetheless we can say that a poem, or any art work, is beautiful when it, by whatever means, brings the *thisness* of the world forcefully to us in a way that does not separate matter from emotion but rather encourages their intermingling.

One might object, however, that "beauty is in the eye of the beholder," anyway. This point is inevitably made whenever one attempts to discuss beauty, and the person who makes it usually seems to think he is being very modern and intellectual. No sentiment, however, could be more dull and conventional than the idea that beauty is subjective.

Both C. S. Lewis, in *The Abolition of Man*, and Dietrich von Hildebrand, in his *Aesthetics*, have shown the foolishness of this position. The latter thinker grounds his view of beauty's objectivity in the very way we use the word *beautiful*:

> The preposition 'for,' as linked organically to something that is merely pleasant, would have a wholly different meaning if it were attached to the predicate 'beautiful.' Normally, we say, 'This color is beautiful, this melody is beautiful'—not 'beautiful for me.' In the exceptional case where we do say this, the word 'for' does not mean that the importance of the color or the melody has its origin in the pleasant effect it has on me; rather, we mean, 'In my opinion, they are beautiful.' In this case, the preposition expresses a relationship to my judgment, which discerns beauty: 'Others may not find them beautiful, but I do.' The importance that is expressed in the term 'beauty' is not in any way expressed by the phrase 'for me,' as it is when I say that something is gratifying for me . . . There

can be no doubt about it: when we see a landscape and exclaim, 'How beautiful it is!' we are referring primarily to a quality of the landscape, not to an effect it has on us.[26]

Hildebrand blames David Hume for modern misperceptions about the nature of beauty. Regardless of who is to blame for the confusion, it is not hard to see Hildebrand's larger point. For instance, I might believe I see a sparrow sitting on a fencepost about 200 yards away, down by the barn. You may say, "no, that is not a sparrow." Our dispute would be about the *accuracy* of my perception, not about the general existence of sparrows. In fact, our disagreement presupposes the existence of sparrows as an objective phenomenon. Similarly, you and I may disagree on what "beauty" refers to—I may find Bach's Brandenburg Concertos beautiful, while you find beauty in Nine Inch Nails—but in the very act of disagreeing over where beauty is found, we have agreed that the word *beauty*, indeed, refers to something. As both Lewis and Hart assert, what happens to us in encountering beauty is a *response* to something objectively present in the object we consider beautiful.[27]

In the Platonic dialogue known as the *Greater Hippias*, Socrates confounds the sophist Hippias by pointing out that, if it is by justice that we are just and by goodness that we are good and by wisdom that we are wise, then it must be by beauty that we are beautiful. He is pointing out that there is something we could call *the beautiful* by which we know individual beauty, be it that of a maiden of a mare or of a piece of pottery. Although the dialogue is unable to determine exactly what *the beautiful* is, Hippias is forced to admit that it must indeed be something. It is not merely in the eye of the beholder. It is left to Christians like Augustine to later discern that *the beautiful*—like *the true* and *the good*—is to be identified with our holy, perfect God: "Late have I loved you, beauty so old and so new: late have I loved you."

B. H. Fairchild's "Beauty" ends with an image of this *given* nature of the beautiful. Having turned, after a long while, from the statue of David, the poet and his wife walk to a window through which they see Florence,

> blazing like miles of uncut wheat, the farthest buildings
> taken in their turn, and the great dome, the way
> the metal roof of the machine shop, I tell her,

---

26. Hildebrand, *Aesthetics*, 16–17.
27. Hart, *Beauty of the Infinite*, 17.

would break into flame late on an autumn day, with such beauty.[28]

Fairchild connects the plains of his youth with the historic city he is visiting, and he sees in both places beauty's power to interrupt, to break into the ordinary and remind us that existence itself is miraculous and that all being points us toward God. Fairchild's metal roof reminds us of how Hopkins, in "God's Grandeur," describes the way the glory of God as seen in creation "will flame out, like shining from shook foil[.]"[29] In the sudden gift of the light over Florence, we are reminded of beauty's resemblance to grace, our unearned and unexpected return into God's presence.

We must be careful to harden our hearts neither to grace nor to beauty. If we must reject sentimentality and a false optimism, it is not because we reject beauty but rather because we insist that the artist and the church take beauty seriously and refuse ever to cheapen it.

---

28. Fairchild, "Beauty," in *Blue Buick*, 69.
29. Hopkins, "God Grandeur," in *Major Works*, 128.

6

Form

What is Verse?

TWO EQUAL AND OPPOSITE errors regarding poetry bounce around in the contemporary world. On the one hand there is the false impression, current among those who have read little of the poetry written in the last hundred years, that something can't be a poem unless it both rhymes and marches along in an anapestic or iambic cadence. On the other, current among those who think themselves better informed about the art of poetry than they in fact are, is the false impression that Whitman and the modernist giants of the twentieth century put to bed once and for all the old regularity of form that marked poetry in the dark ages and now only a rube would write with rhyme and meter. Neither view is a wholly uneducated view, but neither view is wholly educated either.

It is true, of course, that poetry once, for the most part, used to come in the variety we have come to refer to as "formal." That is, we used to call "verse" that species of literature which was organized by patterns often related to syllable and/or emphasis, such as iambic pentameter. This kind of poetry in English often, though not always, made use of rhyme. Poetry of this sort used to be a very regular part of one's primary and secondary education. In the course of gaining an education, one could expect to read, and even memorize, a fair amount of iambic pentameter composed by Shakespeare, Wordsworth, Tennyson, Whittier, and the like. The formal arrangement of the lines into patterns of stressed and unstressed syllables aided greatly in the memorization of verse for the classroom. This sort of literary education was a part of my own experience of middle school in rural Oklahoma in the 1980s, though I understand it has since nearly disappeared.

Meter and form go back far into the ancient roots of Western poetry, with both the Greeks and the Romans developing systems of "prosody" —theorization on the rhythmic arrangement of sound into verse—that focused on syllable length, or *duration*, along with the number of syllables per line. In the Germanic speaking north, such as England, a poetic rhythm developed that centered not on syllable length but rather on "accent," the amount of stress or emphasis put on a syllable relative to the syllables around it. For instance, we say the word *tickle* with the emphasis on the first syllable (if you are unsure what I mean, try saying it with the last syllable emphasized and listen to how odd you sound). The romance languages of southern Europe, derived largely from Latin, however, used accented syllables in a less-pronounced way and thus developed systems of prosody more focused on the number of syllables per line than on patterns of emphasis. When Latin-derived French collided with the Germanic Old English after the Norman Conquest—as we discussed in both the chapter on diction and the chapter on writing the fallen world—the eventual result was a poetic system which counted syllables like the French and arranged them in patterns of stressed and unstressed syllables like the Germanic peoples did in their verse narratives. This combination gives us the familiar "accentual-syllabic" system, in which we count out, for instance, iambic pentameter as ta-*dum* ta-*dum* ta-*dum* ta-*dum* ta-*dum*. That is, ten syllables alternating between unstressed and stressed.[1]

It is true that many of the great poets of the early twentieth century found this form of prosody outdated and stifling. In 1908, the poet and critic T. E. Hulme declared, in his "Lecture on Modern Poetry," that "a shell is a very suitable covering for the egg at a certain period of its career, but very unsuitable at a later age. This seems to me to represent fairly well the state of verse at the present time. . . . [It] has become alive, it has changed from the ancient art of chanting to the modern impressionist, but the mechanism of verse has remained the same. It can't go on doing so. I will conclude, ladies

---

1. For a more thorough history and explication of the English accentual-syllabic system, see the following: Corn, *The Poem's Heartbeat*; Beum and Shapiro, *The Prosody Handbook*; Baer, *Writing Metrical Poetry*; Hollander, *Rhyme's Reason*; and Fussell, *Poetic Form*.

and gentlemen, by saying, the shell must be broken."[2] This position was taken up by literary luminaries like Ezra Pound, William Carlos Williams, and even, for a time, T. S. Eliot. Eliot and Pound perhaps came to regret the slackening they helped introduce to Anglophone poetry, but there was no putting the genie of free verse back in the bottle. Though perhaps slow to take off, free verse came to dominate American poetry by the 1960s.

Yet, we should not exaggerate the victory of free verse. Poets as central to modern poetry as W. B. Yeats, Robert Frost, and W. H. Auden continued to write metrical and rhymed poetry at the height of their creativity and notoriety, even as their contemporaries experimented with other forms of poetic organization. After the second world war, a new generation of "formalists," including renowned poets like Richard Wilbur, Donald Justice, and Anthony Hecht, emerged. Some of these formalist poets were active into the new century. Moreover, in the mid-twentieth century, Elizabeth Bishop, John Berryman, and Robert Lowell proved themselves dazzling in a variety of poetic forms, both free and formal. Then, in the 1980s and '90s, yet another formalist generation, the "new formalists," came to prominence in American poetry through the influence of writers like Annie Finch, Dana Gioia, Mark Jarman, and Andrew Hudgins and in the pages of journals like *The Formalist* and, later, *Measure*.[3] A. E. Stallings, who is one of the twenty-first century's most brilliant and acclaimed poets thus far, is a master of traditional forms, and she continues to dazzle audiences with her felicity for rhythm and rhyme, even as many prominent poetry journals and graduate programs in poetry continue allegiance to free verse as the dominant mode.

Where does that leave the question today? Rather than fighting about whether or not a poem must observe "the rules of verse," we ought to ask what message or view of the world or aesthetic sense is conveyed by whatever shape the poem does take. The second verse of the first chapter of Genesis tells us that in the beginning "[t]he earth was without form and void, and darkness was over the face of the deep. And the Spirit of God was hovering over the face of the waters." It is not hard to see that, over the course of the next two chapters, the Lord brings form, brings a shape that is not just useful or practical but also meaningful and "good" to that formless void. From the Christian viewpoint, a poet does well, whether writing in

---

2. Hulme, "A Lecture on Modern Poetry," in *Selected Writings*, 66–67.

3. A good introduction to this "movement" or "school" is McPhillips, *The New Formalism*.

iambic pentameter or in free verse, to mirror that divinely creative act of bringing order.

Order and Form

Orthodox Christianity insists that, although the world is often disordered by sin, there is an original, persistent, and ultimately triumphant order underlying all of God's creation. When we read in the first chapter of the Gospel of John that "in the beginning was the word," the term we translate as *word* is the Greek *logos*. This word, often used in stoic philosophy, not only means *utterance* or *sign* but also strongly connotes order, reason, and coherence. It is the root of our word *logic*. While the stoics saw this underlying order of the cosmos as an impersonal force, Christianity insists that it is rather a person, Jesus Christ. We are told in Colossians 1:17 that "he is before all things, and in him all things hold together." We may not always be able to see it, but God's world is orderly.

Christian culture has thus associated beauty with order in its long aesthetic tradition. Through the middle ages, *form* and *proportion* were treated as synonymous with beauty.[4] Aesthetic success, in the Christian view, depends to some extent on the ability of the artist to mirror God's orderly creation, sometimes revealing a deeper order beneath the apparent disorder introduced by sin.

Dante's *Divine Comedy* is a prime example of this aesthetic tradition. Although the first third of the poem, the *Inferno*, looks very frankly at the disordering, deforming effects of sin, underlying even the poem's depiction of the deepest pit of hell is an orderly composition. Dante writes lines of eleven syllables (*hendecasyllabics*) in stanzas of three lines with interlocking rhymes, for thirty-three total syllables per stanza, organized into three books, or *canticles*, corresponding with the three realms of the afterlife, as Dante understood them. One can see, without even reading the poem, the poet's fidelity to Trinitarian Christianity. He also adds one introductory canto to the first book, so that the total number of cantos adds up to 100, a number thought to express God's perfection.

Dante is not alone in this view of order. As Stratford Caldecott points out, throughout the history of Christian thought, "[i]t is not simply that numbers can be used as symbols. Numbers have meaning—they *are* symbols. The symbolism is not always merely projected onto them by us; much

---

4. See Eco, *Art and Beauty*, 28–42.

of it is inherent in their nature."[5] Christian thinkers have often emphasized God's use of number in giving order and pattern to creation. This idea exerts a strong influence on the development of our very notion of "poetic form" in the Western world. One old-fashioned term for lines of verse is "numbers." Versification can be a way of seeing, or asserting, order in the world. This may be why the ardently formalist Robert Frost follows up his famous assertion that poetry "begins in delight and ends in wisdom" by defining that wisdom as "a momentary stay against confusion."[6] In short, we expect good poems to exhibit a strong connection between their shape and their content. This is why many poets speak of the form the poem seems to "want" to be during the drafting process.

Some Shapes of Verse

A proper sonnet, for instance, rather than any random conglomeration into fourteen lines of iambic pentameter, is a poem with a particular shape of thought. In the Anglo-American tradition, the sonnet, in fact, usually falls within one of two dominant shapes of thought. When the sonnet was imported into English from Italian in the early sixteenth century, it brought its fairly complex rhyme scheme with it, a scheme appropriate for the rhyme-rich romance language from which it came. Thus, the form of English poem we call the "Italian" or "Petrarchan" sonnet—after its greatest practitioner in Italian, Francesco Petrarca—rhymes as follows:

A
B
B
A
A
B
B
A

C
D
E

---

5. Caldecott, *Beauty for Truth's Sake*, 75.
6. Frost, "The Figure a Poem Makes," in *Collected Prose*, 132.

C
D
E (or a variation thereon)

The first eight lines, or *octave*, set up a problem or establish a situation—usually related to love—which is solved, commented on, or in some other way resolved in the last six lines, or *sestet*. In this way, the rhyme scheme and subdivision of the poem make a particular shape of thought or experience. Not just any poem can be shoved into an Italian sonnet.

We can see this shape of thought in sonnets by the early sixteenth-century diplomat and poet Sir Thomas Wyatt, who, after a diplomatic mission to Italy, returned to England to write deeply personalized English versions of Petrarch's love sonnets. Wyatt's version of Petrarch's 140th sonnet keeps the Italian form:

> The long love that in my thought doth harbor
> And in myn heart doth keep his residence
> Into my face preseth with bold pretence
> And therein campeth spreading his banner.
> She that me learneth to love and suffer
> And wills that my trust and lust's negligence
> Be reigned by reason, shame, and reverence
> With his hardiness taketh displeasure.
> Where with all unto the hearts forest he fleeth
> Leaving his enterprise with pain and cry
> And her him hideth and not appeareth.
> What may I do when my master feareth?
> But in the feld with him to lyve and dye?
> For good is the life ending faithfully.[7]

The turn, or *volta*, that is conventional to the sonnet comes here when the personified love—we are meant to imagine Cupid or *eros*—which has occupied the poet's thought and face, flees into the poet's wild heart. At that moment, the poem seems to turn toward despair. The despairing tone has a full six lines to build toward the noble resignation of the final line. This resignation is the poem's culmination or resting point. The poet's feelings

---

7. Wyatt, "Sonnet #2," in *Poems of Wiat*, 14. I have slightly modernized the spelling for the reader's convenience.

are not crammed into an arbitrary fourteen-line shape but rather are rhetorically congruent with the shape, one could say *the math*, of the poem.

Soon after Wyatt's introduction into English of the Italianate form, his young contemporary, Henry Howard, Earl of Surrey—perhaps finding the Italian form too heavily rhymed for the Germanic English language—offered an innovative English alternative. Thus what we often call the "Shakespearean Sonnet," after its most famous practitioner, though not inventor, rhymes as follows:

    A
    B
    A
    B

    C
    D
    C
    D

    E
    F
    E
    F

    G
    G

The *octave* of the Italian form becomes three *quatrains*—stanzas of four lines—in the English form, stretching out the statement of the problem and delaying the resolution to the final two lines, the rhymed *couplet*. In contrasting Petrarch's *sestet* with Surrey's *couplet*, it is tempting to contrast the more leisurely temperaments of Southern Europe with a more tightly wound Northern temperament. We might even go so far as to see in the two dominant sonnet forms contrasting theologies, the sudden resolution of the couplet mirroring the Protestant emphasis on salvation by grace and the more worked-out Italian *sestet* mirroring a Catholic cooperation of works and grace. Regardless of how we frame the difference, the sonnet provides a clear example of the relationship between shape of poem and shape of thought.

A Poetics of Orthodoxy

The theological/devotional sonnets of John Donne offer a model of this union of form and content. In his "Holy Sonnets," Donne, who when young had used theological metaphors to express his erotic longings, uses erotic metaphors to express his longing for God. In his famous sonnet beginning "Batter my heart three-person'd God," Donne blends the Italian rhyme scheme with Surrey's sudden ending couplet, to heighten the sense of spiritual fraughtness:

> Batter my heart, three-person'd God, for you
> As yet but knock, breathe, shine, and seek to mend;
> That I may rise, and stand, o'erthrow me; and bend
> Your force, to break, blow, burn and make me new.
> I like an usurp'd town, t'another due,
> Labour t'admit you, but oh, to no end,
> Reason, your viceroy in me, me should defend,
> But is captiv'd and proves weak or untrue.
> Yet dearly I love you, and would be loved fain:
> But am betroth'd unto your enemy:
> Divorce me, untie, or break that knot again,
> Take me to you, imprison me, for I
> Except you enthrall me, never shall be free,
> Nor ever chaste except you ravish me.[8]

This is a clear and vivid presentation of salvation by grace alone, and the suddenness of the couplet—augmented by its light and high vowel sounds—emphasizes the poem's theology. In my experience, the most challenging part of working in the English sonnet form is making sure the sudden movement of the couplet is justified in the thought of the poem. Donne meets this challenging brilliantly by appealing to the theological traditions of his Anglican church.

Furthering the deep connection between form and content, Donne also expertly uses metrical substitutions—placing stressed syllables where one would expect an unstressed syllable, or vice-versa—to heighten the sense of struggle and violence in the poem, as in the three consecutive stressed sounds of *"break, blow, burn."* In those hard, stressed sounds—emphasized further by the alliteration—one hears the struggle with God taking place in the poet's heart. The poem thus makes meaning in several ways

---

8. Donne, "Holy Sonnet #10," in *John Donne's Poetry*, 140.

at once, reflecting orthodox Christianity's insistence that the world is rich with meaning, a cosmos of signification. This insistence on meaningfulness is in sharp contrast with modernity's view of an arbitrary universe and an accidental man. Though postmodern, experimental poets have attempted to create aleatory, seemingly accidental, forms of poetry to accommodate a view of the universe as meaningless and blank, most poems written still today, especially in the formal tradition, continue to offer themselves as a brief on behalf of the order of things. Often they do so despite the overtly espoused worldview of their authors.

Of course, the sonnet shape of thought is not limited to expressly theological content or to sonnets written during the age of Renaissance and Reformation. One contemporary poet, R. S. Gywnn, uses the Italian sonnet shape to emphasize the differences in a young man before and after being sent to war:

> Good pulling guards were scarce in high school ball.
> The ones who had the weight were usually slow
> As lumber trucks. A scaled-down wild man, though,
> Like Dennis "Wampus" Peterson, could haul
> His ass around right end for me to slip
> Behind his blocks. Played college ball a year –
> Red-shirted when they yanked his scholarship
> Because he majored, so he claimed, in Beer.
>
> I saw him one last time. He'd added weight
> Around the neck, used worlds like "grunt" and "slope,"
> And said he'd swap his Harley and his dope
> And both balls for a 4-F knee like mine.
> This happened in the spring of '68.
> He hanged himself in 1969.[9]

Here the *volta*, that space between the first eight and the final six lines, contains a multitude of implications, things that Gwynn doesn't have to write. In fact, in trying to express the horrors of war, one always runs the risk of unintentionally trivializing them, of being reductive. Gwynn uses the shape of the sonnet to overcome this problem. He says more by saying less, by letting the shape of the poem speak. In doing so, while he is not

---

9. Gwynn, "Body Bags," in *No Word*, 29.

making any theological statement—isn't in any obvious way talking about God at all—he affirms a sense of order underneath it all. The orderliness of the poem strains against the disorientation of sorrow in a fallen world: "a momentary stay against confusion."

Another example of contemporary excellence in form can be found in Mark Jarman's masterpiece, *The Unholy Sonnets*. Like his obvious predecessor, John Donne, Jarman is a poet given to wrestling with God, yet, even as his sonnets walk us through the wrenching twists and turns of a mind in doubt, his graceful use of form suggests an underlying order. Jarman's poems draw artistic energy from the powerful tension between our experiences in a fallen world and our understanding that God's redemption of that world, and our experience in it, is being accomplished, has been accomplished, and will be accomplished. In the ninth unholy sonnet, for instance, Jarman begins with the stark observation that "Someone is always praying as the plane / Breaks up," and ends by imagining the prayer—and presumably the one who prays it—striking "the blank face of earth, the ocean's face, / The rockhard, rippled face of facelessness."[10] Underneath this anguish is a blank verse sonnet that constantly teeters on the edge of rhyme, suggesting that even when little makes sense to us about the harshness of human life there is still present an unseen *logos*. This underlying order in no way belittles or diminishes the anguish of the poem. Rather, the contrast stirs in us all the more the longing for the perfection of all things in the new heaven and the new earth.

My point is not to recommend any particular sonneteer or iteration of the sonnet form, of course, but rather to stress that, in the best sonnets, form and content correspond, either directly or in a meaningful tension. Further, I would suggest that we find this union of word and thought so satisfying precisely because we live in a reality rooted in the *logos* and we long for that order to become apparent through redemption. Regardless of how consciously we register the cause, we receive real pleasure whenever we experience the logos-affirming coherence of good art.

This pleasure is by no means limited to the sonnet form. Consider Robert Frost's brief and justly famous "Nothing Gold Can Stay":

> Nature's first green is gold,
> Her hardest hue to hold.
> Her early leaf's a flower;

---

10. Jarman, *Unholy Sonnets*, 29.

But only so an hour.
Then leaf subsides to leaf.
So Eden sank to grief,
So dawn goes down to day.
Nothing gold can stay.[11]

Many poems have been written about transience, about the fleeting nature of youth and the passing of time. What makes this one of the best and most memorable? In part, the poem's success is attributable to its marriage of form and content. The lines are in trimeter—six syllable lines with three accented syllables—which is a full four syllables shorter than the standard pentameter line of English verse. Thus, the rhymed couplets happen quickly. The poem happens fast. One has the feeling when reading it aloud that the poem is running by uncontrollably right before our eyes. This is often how life feels, and it is often how we feel about our youth. When form meets content, the poem feels right. It makes sense. Thus, even when the poem focuses on what we cannot control—in this case the passing of time—it simultaneously satisfies our need to feel that there is an order to things. Built into the poem is the sense of *in-betweeness*, the tug between our experiences of a disordered world—the ravages of time the poem so succinctly captures—and our knowledge of and longing for the deeper order of God's creation.

It is possible to identify a shape of thought in most traditional forms of poetry. For instance, certain forms derived from French poetry, like the Villanelle and the Sestina, create an obsessive or desperate pattern in their heavy repetitions, at least in their English iterations. Although the villanelle was for centuries seen as a frivolous and jangling form, modern poets like Dylan Thomas and Elizabeth Bishop saw in the recurring refrain a perfect opportunity to explore obsessive grief and desperate need, as in Thomas's famous "Do Not Go Gentle into that Good Night," a frantic plea to his dying father, or Bishop's moving account of the ubiquity of loss in her poem "One Art."

Looking further back in time, we see that eighteenth-century poets, like Alexander Pope, realized that the measured and even pace of the "heroic couplet," rhymed pairs of iambic pentameter, fit perfectly their confidence in reasonable, moderate modes of discourse. Thus, due to its congruence with the dominant worldview of the time, the heroic couplet

---

11. Frost, "Nothing Gold Can Stay," in *Poetry of Robert Frost*, 222–23.

was the most prominent form of verse during the eighteenth century. Rhyme always makes a strong suggestion of meaning and coherence, which is why Shakespeare often ended scenes of unrhymed verse with a rhymed couplet to cap it off. This natural sense of coherence is also why lawyers, salesmen, and politicians sometimes make use of rhyme to convince us of things that might seem highly doubtful in unadorned prose. The rhymes come so quickly in heroic couplet that we are virtually flooded with a tidy sense of the *just so*.

Contrastingly, both the sixteenth and the nineteenth centuries loved another invention of the Earl of Surrey, blank verse, which, in its sprawling unrhymed lines of iambic pentameter proved perfect for Shakespeare's soliloquies, Milton's theological epic, and Wordsworth's sprawling account of his life in *The Prelude*. In the twentieth century, Robert Frost discovered in blank verse a form congenial to his conversational form of Yankee philosophizing. Any poetry in which a fairly complicated issue needs to be thought through at length right before our eyes or a complex narrative needs to be sustained is a good candidate for blank verse composition.

I don't intend to suggest, of course, that the only good verse is rhymed and metered verse. I cite many admirable free verse poems throughout this book. My point is merely that one measure of a poem is the fit between its form and its content. There are many theories of form for free verse, from William Carlos Williams's "variable foot" to Denise Levertov's "organic form."[12] All attempt to find the connection between what a poems says and how it says it. To put it another way, one might borrow the words of T. S. Eliot: "no verse is free for the man who wants to do a good job."[13]

In a free verse poem, much of the ordering work that would have been done by meter and perhaps rhyme is done by what we tend to call "line breaks." With the ascension of free verse, the question of what gives a line of poetry integrity *as* a line becomes a dominant question in poetics.[14] Here I want to offer just one example of how line breaks can be made to signify, to speak the meaningfulness of the world in a free verse poem. Karen Swenson begins her poem "A Pilgrim into Silence" with these two lines: "The road forks left where we stop on the wind- / scoured edge of ridge; I don't

---

12. For explanations of both, see their respective entries in Gioia et al., eds., *Twentieth-Century American Poetics*.

13. Eliot, "The Music of Poetry," in *On Poetry and Poets*, 31.

14. If the reader is interested in the question of the line, good accounts can be found in two sources in particular: Longenbach, *Art of the Poetic Line*; and Rosko and Vander Zee, eds., *A Broken Thing*.

remember why."¹⁵ It is an easy thing to miss on a first reading, but notice how the line breaks on the connection between "wind" and "scoured," a sharp breaking off that somehow more perfectly conveys the exposed, even sharpened, nature of the ridge. The way the first two lines then come to a complete rest after the short phrase following the semicolon adds to our sense of a pause, along with the pause of the pilgrims in the poem. In short, the experience of the poem is written into the shape of the poem, which gratifies the reader by appealing, mostly unconsciously, to our need for a cosmos that makes sense.

In free verse much of the consonance between form and subject matter lies also in the length of the line. The iambic pentameter line may no longer reign supreme in English-language poetry, but its ten syllables still set the standard length for the poetic line. In other words, any line of poetry between roughly eight and twelves syllables will be fairly inconspicuous as regards length. A poem with an average of ten lines per syllable will read a lot like blank verse, and many poets who tend toward narrative work, like B. H. Fairchild, will often blur the line between blank verse and free verse in inconspicuous line lengths. Any line notably shorter or longer than ten syllables, however, will be conspicuous. Thus artistic coherence demands that the poem's subject, tone, and mood work in tandem with the dominant length of line in the poem.

The long free verse line is best thought of as the "prophetic line." There are both physical and historical reasons for thinking of it in this way. Physically, since we tend to take breaths at the end of the line, the prophetic line creates a sensation of literal breathlessness. To read the long line is to inhabit the body of the street corner prophet, to declaim. Historical association amplifies this association, since the most renowned practitioners of the lengthy line in English—William Blake and Walt Whitman—take their inspiration in large part from the King James translations of the Old Testament prophets. Almost any lines from Whitman's *Leaves of Grass* will demonstrate this association. Here, for instance, are some lines from section sixteen of "Song of Myself":

> I am of old and young, of the foolish as much as the wise, Regardless of others, ever regardful of others, Maternal as well as paternal, a child as well as a man, /

---

15. Swenson, "A Pilgrim into Silence," in *Pilgrim into Silence*, 63.

> Stuff'd with the stuff that is coarse and stuff'd with the stuff that is fine,
>
> One of the Nation of many nations, the smallest the same and the largest the Same, /
>
> A Southerner soon as a Northerner, a planter nonchalant and hospitable down by the Oconee I live....[16]

In his prophetic assertion of a union with all the cosmos, Whitman uses here lines ranging from fourteen to twenty-nine syllables. The large line matches the large vision, and, while the sentiment may be more pantheist than orthodox, the union of form and meaning resonates with our expectations of a coherence. For this reason, poets who follow Whitman in the declamatory mode, for instance Allen Ginsberg, rely heavily upon the visionary resonances of the long line.

The contrasting short line we might best refer to as the "ontological line." I call this line *ontological* because it tends not to focus on broad visions but rather to take a close look at what particularly *is*. Ontology is the branch of philosophy that considers being itself, that asks questions related to existence and reality. The best example of the ontological line is Williams's "The Red Wheelbarrow," which I quoted in a previous chapter. When students ask me what this poem "really" means, I ask them to consider the possibility that the poem is simply directing our attention to some of the things that exist: the wheelbarrow, the rain water, the chickens. The short line is particularly suited for this ontological purpose because the frequent reoccurrence of line endings cause frequent pauses in the reading, which results in the sensation of working carefully, step by step, down the page through the poem. Rather than the Bible, the historical precedent here is far Eastern poetry, particularly the haiku and how it has been traditionally translated into English in three lines of five, seven, and five syllables. If one were to look for an inheritor of Williams's ontological line, Ginsberg's friends and associates Gary Snyder and Robert Creeley would both make good examples.

Because we know, on some level, that the world is ordered, even when that order is obscured, we seek that order in our art. Poems that achieve a high level of aesthetic success, whether on the scale of the *Divine Comedy* or on that of "Nothing Gold Can Stay," thus reflect that orderliness, though sometimes in ways that are not immediately apparent. It may be through

---

16. Whitman, "Song of Myself," in *Leaves of Grass*, 39.

the use of traditional form or it may be through strategies in free verse to match the tone and view of the poem with the length of line, but in some way great poetry will suggest a coherence beneath the apparent incoherence. It will offer itself as Frost's "momentary stay against confusion."

7

Metaphor

Meaning and Enchantment

WELL INTO HIS ADVENTURES as told in C. S. Lewis's *The Voyage of the Dawn Treader*, Eustace Scrubb meets a retired star. That is, not a movie star or a rock star, but an actual star, from the sky. The star, who calls himself Ramandu, is living with his beautiful daughter on an island far out in the seas beyond Narnia. The formerly dull and nasty Eustace, essentially transformed by his encounter with Aslan but still skeptical in his habits of mind, explains to Ramandu that, "[i]n our world . . . a star is a huge ball of flaming gas." The wise old star responds, "Even in your world, my son, that is not what a star is but only what it is made of."[1] As he so often does, Lewis invites us to consider that there are more things in heaven and earth than are dreamed of in our, often unconsciously adopted, materialist philosophies.

The difference between Eustace's view and the way of seeing represented by Ramandu can be understood in terms of what is sometimes called "disenchantment." The "enchanted" world is a world rich with meaning, with signification. In an "enchanted" world, nothing is ever just the sum total of its material parts. In this sense, then, "enchantment" does not refer to some nefarious magic, such as a deluding spell cast by a wicked wizard. Rather, in this sense, the enchanted world is a cosmos in which all things gesture beyond themselves to a system of correspondences, connections

---

1. Lewis, *The Voyage of the Dawn Treader*, 522.

Metaphor

that make sense of the world by pointing to a meaning larger than what is at first apparent. Umberto Eco describes the enchanted cosmos as envisioned by medieval thought:

> In a symbolical universe, everything is in its proper place because everything answers to everything else. In such a harmonious system, the serpent is homogeneous with the virtue of prudence; and yet the same serpent can symbolize Satan. It was a kind of polyphony of signs and references. Christ and His divinity are symbolized by a vast number and variety of creatures, each signifying His presence in a different place—in heaven, on mountain-tops, in the fields, the forests, and the seas. The symbols used included the lamb, the dove, the peacock, the ram, the gryphon, the rooster, the lynx, the palm-tree, even a bunch of grapes: a polyphony of images.[2]

Eco refers to this world of layered and multiple signification as the world of "universal allegory."[3] Good allegory is not a wooden one-to-one correspondence in which a writer says one thing but *really* means another, a sort of literary Candy Land. Nor is good allegory the simple denial of a plain and literal sense in favor of some esoteric "hidden" sense. Real allegory depends on the literal in order to reach the symbolic. True allegory is a rich opening up of meaning onto meaning and meaning. For Christians before the modern age, the world was an allegory, rich with meaning. This is the world to which poetry, particularly through metaphorical language, can return us. This is the world in which good poetry is grounded.

The Story of Secularization

Gnostics ancient and modern see the created world around us—the *cosmos* or universe—as, at best, beneath their interest and as, at worst, inherently evil. Thus, they do not heed the words of Romans 1:20: "For his invisible attributes, namely, his eternal power and divine nature, have been clearly perceived, ever since the creation of the world, in the things that have been made. So they are without excuse." Orthodox Christians over the centuries have spoken of "The Book of Nature" as a metaphor for God's meaning-filled creation. In our time, however, the gnostic view that sees matter as *mere* matter has crept into the way even Christians conceptualize the world

---

2. Eco, *Art and Beauty*, 56.
3. Eco, *Art and Beauty*, 56.

around us. But, if poetry can bring us back to inhabiting the world as embodied beings, it can also help us to see the connection between the physical world and transcendent meaning. Good poetry does exactly that, not through high-handed directions to observe the transcendent but, rather, through the abundant use of metaphor.

The Western mind's loss of the enchanted world is a complicated story, one told in great detail in philosopher Charles Taylor's magnum opus, *A Secular Age*. Taylor describes how, over time, the Western mind-set shifted from a view of the cosmos as "a universe of ordered signs, in which everything has a meaning" to a view of the universe as "a silent but beneficent machine," a change he calls "the mechanization of the world picture."[4] We can think of this change as the replacement of Dante's allegorical view of the world as expressed in the *Divine Comedy* by Isaac Newton's mechanical view in the *Principia Mathematica*. I'm not, of course, suggesting that Newton, or science more generally, is *wrong*. I am pointing out a shift from one way of being right to another, a shift away from one true form of understanding to a contrasting framework, which is a move away from poetry —including the biblical poetry of the Psalms and prophets—and toward science as the Western world's primary way of articulating an understanding of the universe.

This shift spawned the modern privileging of reason over imagination, along with the backlash of imagination both in nineteenth-century Romanticism and in contemporary postmodernism. The dominance of reason over imagination in intellectual life, along with the abuses of the imagination in extreme forms of romanticism and postmodernism, have left the church unsure of what to do with the imagination. This is certainly one reason the contemporary church has such a troubled relationship with the arts. We have lost our sense of the sanctified imagination that can show us a world of deep meaning and permanent truth.

At the end of the *Divine Comedy*, Dante describes a beatific vision of God in heaven, in which the poet discerns "Bound up with love together in one volume / What through the universe in leaves is scattered[.]"[5] Dante is confident that, even if we can in this life read the world only as scattered pages (or "leaves"), viewed from heaven the universe is a fully legible book. From the viewpoint of heaven, the world is a book that makes perfect sense and is fully coherent. We may often have trouble discerning meaning, but

---

4. Taylor, *A Secular Age*, 98.
5. Dante, *Paradiso* XXXIII.86–87.

meaning is always there. Today, even Christians, however, are far more likely to describe God as a "designer" than as an "author." As Mike Cosper says, "We didn't choose to feel this way. It's simply the world of ideas we inhabit, a thousand stories told and repeated about how the world works. Christians and non-Christians alike are disenchanted because we're all immersed in a world that presents a material understanding of reality as the plausible and grown-up way of thinking."[6] Even among those professing a belief in the supernatural—and despite, by the way, the weirdness of contemporary theoretical physics—Newton's machine universe has become the dominant metaphor by which we understand the nature of things.

Taylor and others lay part of the blame for modern disenchantment at the feet of the Protestant Reformers, and this is perhaps a fair charge.[7] It is worth noting, however, that the thoroughly Protestant poet Edmund Spenser, in his great sixteenth-century epic *The Faerie Queene*, is as committed to the allegorical view of the world as is Dante. Protestants may be more susceptible to disenchantment than are Catholics, but that doesn't mean that all varieties of Protestantism are necessarily disenchanted or that Protestantism is inevitably a cause of secularization.

Whatever the cause, by the time we get to John Milton's monumental Protestant epic in the late seventeenth century, *Paradise Lost*, there is very little direct allegory left, the only allegorical characters being his Sin and Death, who make merely brief appearances. Indeed, reading the philosophical treatise most likely by Milton, *On Christian Doctrine*, one wonders if the poet's persistent literal-mindedness and hyper-rationality is partly to blame for his susceptibility to the Arian heresy. In this way, Milton could be called one of the first thoroughly modern men. Milton's contemporary, the Puritan John Bunyan, while theologically insightful and generally more orthodox, writes a kind of allegory that is at first relatively rigid and simplistic, signaling perhaps the end of the richly textual universe with his rigid attempt to create a univocal universe, at least until late in *The Pilgrim's Progress*, when we come to the more mysterious account of death in the form of a river-crossing. On the whole, as delightful and instructive as it can be, *The Pilgrim's Progress* is not so much the last gasp of the allegorical worldview as it is its stiffened corpse.

---

6. Cosper, *Recapturing the Wonder*, 10.

7. For a good start on defending Protestantism against that charge, while still acknowledging the cogency of Taylor's argument, see Michael Horton, "The Enduring Power of the Christian Story," in Hansen, ed., *Our Secular Age*.

There is no doubt that the mechanized universe has brought us much benefit in scientific advances. The kind of material inquiry made possible by the scientific revolution has given much of the world longer and more comfortable lives. That is something for which to be grateful. But we, especially we Christians, must also feel some sense of loss when contemplating the disenchantment to which we are subject. Viewing the world as a machine has brought us a lifestyle more comfortable than any ancient emperor could aspire to. It has brought us an astounding lifespan and amazing opportunities for knowledge, travel, and good works. It has also, however, brought us a world that often seems devoid of meaning. A world that is, as Hamlet says, "weary, flat, and stale." Perhaps thinking of Hamlet's words, Charles Taylor speaks of "a wide sense of malaise at the disenchanted world, a sense of it as flat, empty, a multiform search for something within, or beyond it, which could compensate for the meaning lost with transcendence[.]"[8] Secularization has fostered even in the church a secular habit of mind, a tendency to live our lives by the compass of materialist thinking even as we profess belief in a transcendent God. Without the book of the world to read, our lives are impoverished of meaning.

The Mystery of Metaphor in the Christian Life

We experience disenchantment as a loss because God wants better for us. Through Holy Scripture, God calls us to live in a cosmos of signification. "In the beginning was the Word," says John 1:1, and the Greek word translated as "word" is *logos*, a term that suggests not just the speech act but also the reason behind it. That is to say, in the *logos* meaning and speech are united in something we might call *signification*. We are thus informed that, not only is there a "meaning to it all," but also that this meaning is not a *what* but a *who*. Psalm 19:2 tells us that "Day to day pours out speech, / and night to night reveals knowledge," a picture of a world fairly buzzing with meaning. The psalmist goes on to revel in metaphor, in verse five describing a sun "which comes out like a bridegroom leaving his chamber / and, like a strong man, runs its course with joy." God calls us to see the world as packed with meaning, a living book, a world of metaphor.

He calls us, too, to see our relationship with him in the context of deep forms of truth. It is perhaps helpful to distinguish between the analytical and rhetorical tool of "analogy" and the deeper suggestiveness of metaphor.

8. Taylor, *A Secular Age*, 302.

If we treat the biblical insistence that God is our father, for instance, as a mere analogy, then it is informative about God but not ultimately true. Analogy works by distinction, giving us two things that are alike in a limited way but are not really connected. But if we treat the fatherhood of God as a metaphor, then we can live secure with the deep mystery of his love for us. Analogy asserts a similarity, but metaphor asserts a correspondence, a deeper connection that runs through all things. This deep connection is why metaphor gives such pleasure and why it is a crucial part of poetry.

I should note here that I am using "metaphor" not in the strictest sense it is used in rhetoric, but to mean generally metaphorical language, including simile, personification, and the like. I would also include analogical interpretation as it is understood by theologians as being more in the camp of metaphor than of *mere* analogy. By "metaphor" I mean any connection between two things made through language and on a level deeper, more mysterious and meaningful, than the comparison of convenience I am calling mere analogy.

One of the great philosophers of language, Paul Ricoeur, asserts a profound relationship between metaphor and truth when he describes metaphor as a "blossoming forth" of deeper meaning.[9] To elaborate on this, he says, "Can one not say that the strategy of language at work in metaphor consists in obliterating the logical and established frontiers of language, in order to bring to light new resemblances the previous classification kept us from seeing? In other words, the power of metaphor would be to break an old categorization, in order to establish new logical frontiers on the ruins of their forerunners."[10] Metaphor makes us rethink the categories by which we organize our world. It causes us to look deeper and reconsider what reality is, not to see wrongly but to see more deeply. Perhaps indebted to Samuel Taylor Coleridge's famous view of the imagination as a way of knowing about the world, Ricoeur argues for "the possibility that metaphor is not limited to suspending natural reality, but that in opening meaning up on the imaginative side it also opens it towards a dimension of reality that does not coincide with what ordinary language envisages under the name of natural reality."[11] Metaphor is a way of seeing more deeply.

Ricoeur argues that metaphor creates a new vision of reality, but he is not espousing a postmodern relativism. Metaphor deepens rather than

---

9. Ricoeur, *Rule of Metaphor*, 43.
10. Ricoeur, *Rule of Metaphor*, 197.
11. Ricoeur, *Rule of Metaphor*, 211.

alters our vision, more like a pair of good spectacles than like a psychedelic drug. He is careful to keep metaphor within the framework of what is sometimes called the "correspondence concept of truth," which insists that anything we call truth corresponds with objective reality.[12] He isn't suggesting that metaphor bends truth beneath our will. He is suggesting that metaphor opens for us a vision of truth really there but unavailable on what we call the strictly literal view of the world. Metaphor re-enchants, not by casting a veil over our eyes like an evil wizard in a fairy tale but by removing from our sight the veil reductive modernity has placed there.

The great American novelist and essayist Walker Percy says something similar in an essay on the wonder of accidental metaphors, metaphors blundered into. For Percy, all metaphor entails a wonderful "element of outlandishness."[13] I believe this "outlandishness" should remind us of the holy excesses of the spirit, the abundance of a God who is not just holy but "holy, holy, holy." Percy tells how, in his youth, he frequently heard a Seeburg brand record player referred to as a "seabird." He asserts that the "mistake" results in a metaphor that reveals something about the object we might have otherwise missed. He insists, however, that finding a "seabird" in a Seeburg is an act not of invention but of discovery: "There is a danger at this point in my being misunderstood as trying to strike a blow for the poetic against the technical, feeling against science, and on the usual aesthetic grounds. But my intention is quite the reverse. I mean to call attention to the rather remarkable fact that in conceiving the machine under the 'wrong' symbol *seabird*, we should somehow know it better, conceive it in a more plenary fashion, have more immediate access to it, than under its descriptive title."[14] Percy insists that metaphor doesn't twist reality but rather illuminates it. We get closer to the nature of the thing by seeing it as another thing. This "more immediate access" is what Paul Ricoeur refers to as a "blossoming" and what Charles Taylor calls "re-enchantment."

One reason, by the way, Christians ought to be alert to the importance of metaphor is because we should have a biblical view of the importance of the sacraments of the church. I belong to a denomination that takes the symbolic view of the Lord's Supper, yet I hate to hear communion explained as *just* a symbol. The words *just* or *mere* as applied to the symbolic import of the bread and the wine (usually in our case, juice) misses entirely the

---

12. Ricoeur, *Rule of Metaphor*, 254.
13. Percy, *Message in the Bottle*, 66.
14. Percy, *Message in the Bottle*, 68.

importance of metaphor in the biblical view of the world. Symbols matter to God and ought to be treated with reverence by God's children. We Christians find ourselves with a range of beliefs, running from Catholic transubstantiation through Luther's consubstantiation and Calvin's pneumatic presence to Zwingli and the Baptists' concept of symbol. The very existence of such debates acknowledges the deep mystery of metaphor. We are forced to acknowledge the bottomlessness of communion's meaning, even as we debate vigorously and firmly adhere each to our own positions. Whatever our view of their nature, to dismiss communion or baptism as *mere* symbols is to surrender entirely to the materialist, disenchanted view of the world: to be effectively secularized. Let us affirm that baptism and the Lord's supper are more than mere analogy in the rhetorical sense. Let us proclaim them wonderfully symbolic, beautiful and profound metaphors, and then debate what we mean by that.

Poetry Versus Secularization

The good news is that, while the sort of total allegorical world pictures constructed in *The Divine Comedy* and *The Faerie Queene* have largely disappeared from our literature, poetry of all kinds carries embers of its fire in the use of metaphorical language. One of contemporary poetry's best-selling poets, Billy Collins, claims that "[t]he philosophical motive behind poetic comparisons is, then, to move the world closer to the condition of harmony, ultimately an absolute harmony in which all things are connected, a simile-and-metaphor-riddled world where everything is like everything else."[15] In this view, poetry can be a sort of rear-guard effort against disenchantment.

To assert a meaningful connection between all things, a "simile-and-metaphor-riddled world," is to assert the creation-affirming "pancalistic" view which Umberto Eco describes as a crucial part of the Christian vision. Thus, metaphor is another means of combating the gnostic dismissal of matter. If God has authored creation, filled it with signification, then we must treat God's book—the book of nature, or the book of matter—as precious. We must not decline to read it.

One way poetic metaphor helps us to read the world deeply is through what we might call its "visual function" of clarifying an image. When

15. Collins, "Poetry, Pleasure, and the Hedonist Reader," in Citino, ed., *The Eye of the Poet*, 20–21.

I think of metaphor, for instance, I think of Richard Wilbur's wonderful poem "Love Calls Us to the Things of this World," for, like love, metaphor calls us to the things of this world. For instance, when Tania Runyan, in her poem "My Daughter's Hands," asks, "When did you hatch these pink birds / that alight on everything in the house?" the metaphor makes us see the child's hands not just more clearly but more *truly* than would be possible had she just said, "when did your hands get so busy?"[16] We might borrow Ricoeur's phrase and say that the hands "blossom forth" in *birdness*. In turn, our wonder at God's creation blossoms forth in appreciation.

Go back to Frost's "Birches," and consider how much more vivid the image of the bent over birches is once he compares them to girls drying their hair:

> You may see their trunks arching in the woods
> Years afterwards, trailing their leaves on the ground
> Like girls on hands and knees that throw their hair
> Before them over their heads to dry in the sun.[17]

Through the simile, Frost gives the birches more fully to us. We see the trees as more truly what they are because we see them in deep connection to something which they plainly are not.

A literary critical vocabulary speaks of metaphor as composed of two equal parts: the tenor and the vehicle. The tenor is the thing the poet wants to get at, the main thing. The vehicle is the means by which the poet describes the thing he or she wants to describe. For instance, in Joe Weil's poem "First Memory" he describes basement "pipes like soldiers / at Valley Forge— / wrapped in rags to keep them from / freezing."[18] The tenor is the pipes; the vehicle is the soldiers at Valley Forge. The best metaphors can bring both the tenor and the vehicle into sharper focus. Somehow, after reading the poem, we see both the pipes and the soldiers Weil is comparing them to more truly. This sort of connection need not be constant in a poem, but poetry can't go for long without it. Even Homer's restrained and relentlessly narrative verse is frequently punctuated with his famous "Homeric similes" in which he connects his characters to the natural world through metaphoric language, comparing the Greek and Trojan warriors to lions, bulls, snakes, and even boulders.

16. Runyan, "My Daughter's Hands," in *A Thousand Vessels*, 14.
17. Frost, "Birches," in *Poetry of Robert Frost*, 121–22.
18. Weil, "First Memory," in *Great Grandmother Light*, 34.

Sometimes a vehicle can so clearly give us the essence of the tenor that the tenor itself hardly needs to figure directly in the poem. The tenor becomes nowhere and everywhere. Such is the case in Richard Wilbur's beautiful poem "A Simile for Her Smile."[19] In this twelve-line poem, only two lines contain direct reference to the tenor, the beloved's smile. Yet, how real, how full of being Wilbur has made this particular smile through his use of metaphors suggestive of peace, brightness, and smoothness. It is, in fact, a more truly particular smile, more the smile of an individual, though we don't know of whom, than it would be if he tried simply to describe it directly. By becoming something else, the smile is more fully itself. Such a blossoming through metaphor makes the world more wonderful to us, or, rather, helps us better see the wonder that is there. We are re-enchanted by the poem. A little time spent with Wilbur's collected works will quickly convince one that this master American poet saw re-enchanting the world as one of the modern poet's top priorities, which is why his beautiful, hopeful work is often juxtaposed to the cheap cynicism of much modern verse.

This trick of metaphor, of making things more themselves by changing them to something else, reminds us that it is not just metaphor's ability to clarify image that makes it a powerful force for enchantment. It is also its insistence on the powerful but mysterious connection between things. That is to say, it is the very existence of metaphor that re-enchants. In his poem, "The Hereafter," for instance, Andrew Hudgins describes his feeling about death: "For so long I have thought of us as nails / God drives into the oak floor of this world, / it's hard to comprehend the hammer turned / to claw me out."[20] The astounding connection between two seemingly unrelated things is exciting in and of itself. We think to ourselves, "I never would have thought of it that way, but, yes!" As Aristotle says, "Liveliness is specially conveyed by metaphor, and by the further power of surprising the hearer; because the hearer expected something different, his acquisition of the new ideas impresses him all the more. His mind seems to say, 'Yes, to be sure; I never thought of that.'"[21] We take pleasure in the feeling of having discovered a deep correspondence beneath the surface of the seemingly disparate things of this world. In the very act of disrupting our sense of the world, metaphor makes more sense of the world.

---

19. Wilbur, "A Simile for Her Smile," in *Collected Poems*, 405.
20. Hudgins, "The Hereafter," in *American Rendering*, 95–96.
21. Aristotle, *Rhet.* III.11. 1412a.

A Poetics of Orthodoxy

This "re-enchantment" implicit in all metaphor is made almost explicit in Jeanne Murray Walker's wonderful poem "Gesture Upwards," the title of which alone suggests poetry's power to return our sense of transcendence. The poem begins with the limitations of the disenchanted world and then, little by little and image by image, works to return correspondence, or meaning, to our vision of nature. Here is the poem in its entirety:

> I have promised to pray for a friend,
> the way one promises when there are no solutions.
> Here in Vermont the cold is slowing things down—
> the way a squad car parked along the shoulder
> slows traffic. The birches are migrating
> to precincts of yellow. From there
> they'll take their permanent leave.
> I pull into a lane to study how they do it.
> Beside the road a cat stretches, pouring herself
> towards her paws. Birds scatter, fanning out
> as if flung into the sky, as if someone
> wants to demonstrate the physics of motion,
> nothing about bones and muscles, just a flawless
> gesture upwards. The leaves float down so slowly
> it feels as if my car is sinking under water.
> I am a fish, watching the sea turn
> gold. Like the sole of a foot, a yellow leaf
> steps on the windshield, then another,
> and another—feet, walking on water.[22]

All good poems drop the reader off somewhere other than where he or she was picked up, and this poem takes us on a journey from disenchantment (prayer seen as only the last, and probably ineffectual, recourse) to miracle and to the presence of the Christ who cares and intercedes so that our prayers may be answered. The poem begins by making prayer seem fruitless and then, through metaphor, restores us to a world in which prayer can be expected to be efficacious. The re-enchantment that ends with the Christocentric image of feet walking on water begins as early as the comparison of the changing season to the effects of a traffic cop. We can, of course, see how the two are alike, but Walker is making more than an analogy; she is

---

22. Walker, "Gesture Upwards," in *New Tracks*, 18.

reaching through the similarity to suggest deep connections in the world. Metaphor may begin in analogy, but it ends in mystery. Her metaphors gesture toward a world that coheres in more than just the physical sense, a world that is more than accident. She is preparing us to see Jesus in the poem's final image. In turn, the image prepares us to see Jesus in the world.

There is much fine craft in this poem. Its rhythms and its images are masterful. Yet, it would not have quite the same re-enchanting effect without its metaphors. Let's "decompose" this poem to imagine it without the metaphors:

> I have promised to pray for a friend,
> the way one promises when there are no solutions.
> Here in Vermont the cold is slowing things down.
> The birches are turning yellow.
> I pull into a lane to look at them.
> Beside the road a cat stretches.
> Birds scatter, fanning out.
> The leaves float down slowly.

With the metaphors gone, the hope is gone. There are still some lovely images, but they don't seem to gesture far beyond themselves. The de-metaphorized poem is a secularized poem. The poem without its astounding connections offers only loss, with no hope of compensation in a more meaningful order of things. The falling of the leaves now suggests only death, no miracle to translate the loss into hope of resurrection.

Metaphor in Proper Measure

And yet prominent voices in poetry have urged us toward just such a disenchanted world. When I was a college freshman, just starting to learn my poetic craft, I attended a reading by the prominent, and by then aging, beat poet Allen Ginsberg. Ginsberg was the most prominent, and I think most talented, of the "Beat Poets" who stormed the literary world in the middle of the twentieth century, starting a countercultural artistic movement that is still sending its ripples through American culture today. By a strange turn of luck, I ended up at diner with the famous poet, who was gracious enough to read and comment on some of my early efforts at poetry. Ginsberg greatly influenced my youthful poems, and—though I have come to contrasting conclusions with his regarding religion, politics, and morality—I still admire the inventiveness and energy of his poetry. At the time, I was star-struck, and I was thrilled to hear his thoughts on my work. I was, however, shocked when Ginsberg marked through every simile and metaphor in my poems. "Just write exactly what you see," he said.

Even then, I was surprised that this visionary poet—who wrote some of the most psychedelic and mystical poems of the mid-twentieth century and who frequently encouraged a poetics based on meditation and Eastern spirituality—would tell me to stick to the literal. I now see that Ginsberg was following his models, the modernist generation before him, particularly William Carlos Williams, who had been an early friend and encourager of young Ginsberg.

Looking at Williams's most famous work, such as "The Red Wheel Barrow" and "This is Just to Say," one sees no metaphorical language, only direct presentation. Most modernists saw their work as a correction of the aesthetic excesses of their Victorian predecessors, a perspective which led them to distrust metaphorical language as mere ornamentation. Ezra Pound says, "I believe that the proper and perfect symbol is the natural object, that if a man uses 'symbols' he must so use them that their symbolic function does not obtrude; so that *a* sense, and the poetic quality of the passage, is not lost to those who do not understand the symbol as such, to whom, for instance, a hawk is a hawk."[23] The modernists produced wonderfully focused poems which scraped away a lot of Victorian excess and which, as we saw in the first chapter, restored a proper focus on imagery to modern poetry. We might say, however, that a world in which a hawk is *only* a hawk is a disenchanted world, a world under the spell of modernist rationalism and the reductive philosophy of positivism, only interested in the empirical and the measurable. Contrastingly, to Gerard Manly Hopkins, the "Windhover," a falcon, is a picture of Christ.

I suspect this insistent literalness of modernity is why Williams disliked Eliot's "The Love Song of J. Alfred Prufrock," with its elaborate similes and metaphors. Williams says of the poem, "I had a violent feeling that Eliot had betrayed what I believed in. He was looking backward; I was looking forward. He was a conformist, with wit, learning which I did not possess."[24] I think greater distance may give us the opportunity to judge more accurately who is the true "conformist," Williams who, as brilliant as he is, goes so easily along with the tide of modern secularization or Eliot who bucks it

---

23. Pound, "A Retrospect," in *Literary Essays*, 9.
24. Williams, *I Wanted to Write*, 30.

to bet everything on transcendence, converting to Christianity shortly after the publication of his groundbreaking poem *The Wasteland*. Nonetheless, Williams goes on to charge that Eliot is un-American in his looking backwards to a time when metaphors and similes were as common as doilies on the parlor furniture.

False Metaphor

As time has shown, few would follow Williams in his low estimation of Eliot's brilliant poem, but Williams and Pound were right to be suspicious of the merely ornamental use of metaphor, if foolish to throw the baby out with the metaphorical bathwater. When metaphorical language is divorced from deep significance, when it is tacked onto a poem rather than integral to it, it cheapens, rather than deepens, our sense of the meaningfulness of the cosmos.

Take, for instance, the extended metaphor in Henry Wadsworth Longfellow's "The Children's Hour."[25] As the poet sits in his study at twilight, he hears overhead "the patter of little feet" as his three daughters descend the stair and interrupt his quiet contemplation. He imagines this domestic interruption as an invasion:

> A sudden rush from the stairway,
> A sudden raid from the hall!
> By three doors left unguarded
> They enter my castle wall!

So far, the metaphor is not bad, perhaps even offering some antidote to the sentimentality of the previous stanzas. It is, at the very least, an amusing scenario: the serious poet-scholar in his study invaded by his impish children. The metaphor brings a winsomeness to the poem thus far.

Longfellow, however, stretches the metaphor to absurdity in the next stanza:

> They climb up into my turret
> O'er the arms and back of my chair;
> If I try to escape, they surround me;
> They seem to be everywhere.

---

25. Longfellow, "The Children's Hour," in *Poems of Longfellow*, 277–78.

The overstretched metaphor muddies, rather than clarifies, the image. Is the turret the chair or is it the poet himself? For me, it is impossible to read these lines without picturing a cartoon scenario in which the children scale a man who has a stone tower for his torso and head. I don't think this helps me to see the world in any clearer or deeper way. The absurdity is compounded in a later stanza:

> I have you fast in my fortress,
> And will not let you depart,
> But put you down into the dungeon
> In the round-tower of my heart.

Apparently, Longfellow has become the Greek god Saturn who devours his own children. It is hard not to imagine the resulting case of heartburn. Of course, the connotations of "dungeon" are so completely at odds with the saccharine sentiment of the poem as to render the metaphor meaningless. This incoherence comes to a head in the final stanza:

> And there will I keep you forever,
> Yes, forever and a day,
> Till the walls shall crumble to ruin,
> And moulder in dust away!

When images of dungeons are combined with "moulder" and "dust," we are left with three skeletons chained to a crumbling wall in the poet's castle/corpse. As Aristotle noted, "Metaphors, like epithets, must be fitting, which means that they must fairly correspond to the thing signified: failing this, their inappropriateness will be conspicuous: the want of harmony between two things is emphasized by their being placed side by side."[26] This medieval horror is hardly the picture of domestic sweetness Longfellow set out to capture. In an attempt to add ornament, he pushed the metaphor too hard, stretching it beyond mystery into absurdity, and thus ended up with a poem too clever by half.

This aesthetic flaw is not unique to the nineteenth century. It was foolishly encouraged as early as 1589 in George Puttenham's *The Art of English Poesie*. Puttenham argues by means of an extended analogy:

> cannot our vulgar Poesie shew it selfe either gallant or gorgeous, if any lymme be left naked and bare and not clad in his kindly clothes and colurs, such as may convey them somewhat out of sight, that is

---

26. Aristotle, *Rhet.* III.2. 1405a.

> from the common course of ordinary speech and capacitie or the vulgar judgement, and yet being artificially handled must needs yeld it much more bewtie and commendation. This ornament we speake of is given to it by figures and figurative speaches, which be the flowers, as it were, and colouurs that a Poet setteth upon his language of arte, as the embroderer doth his stone and perle or passements of gold upon the stuffe of a Princely garment[.][27]

Puttenham seems to see nothing to metaphor beyond pure ornamentation, and he positively encourages its abuse through excess. Sentiments such as this influenced Renaissance sonneteers to pile metaphors into their poems merely as a form of decoration, a practice the eminently sensible William Shakespeare parodied in his sonnet #130: "My mistresses eyes are nothing like the sun."

Yet a deeper use of metaphor extends well back into the poetic tradition. Aristotle proclaimed that "the greatest thing by far is to be a master of metaphor. It is the one thing that cannot be learnt from others; and it is also a sign of genius, since a good metaphor implies an intuitive perception of the similarity in dissimilars."[28] Aristotle, no doubt, had in mind the force of the Homeric simile, which later filtered down from Homer through Virgil and became a distinctly Christian way of seeing in Dante. Perhaps Aristotle is right that real genius with metaphor can't be taught, but an appreciation for the power of metaphor can certainly be cultivated in both readers and writers. As all elements of art in writing, reading the masters of the art is the best way to develop one's taste for and understanding of metaphor.

And to so develop one's metaphorical sense is crucial work. It is part of developing the Christian imagination. That metaphor can be abused to the point of being ripe for parody is no reason for the writer to avoid it. When used well, metaphor has an inherently re-enchanting effect. All good poetry, thus, stands athwart secularization yelling stop, to adapt William F. Buckley's famous definition of conservativism.

First Corinthians 13:12 tells us that in this life "we see in a mirror dimly" but someday we will see clearly. Metaphor begins that process of seeing more clearly. The true purpose of allegory, simile, and other metaphoric type figures of speech is not to obscure meaning but to magnify it, clarify it, and embody it. That is the reason we need metaphor in poetry, and that is the standard by which we judge its execution. When metaphor

27. Puttenham, *Arte of English Poesie*, 142–43.
28. Aristotle, *Poet.* 22. 1459a.

becomes a habit of mind for us, we are less likely to reduce God's beautiful book to a utilitarian machine. When we become more comfortable with metaphor, we become more alert to the depths of God's creation and of God's creativeness. Any good metaphor can be a step toward worshipping the one true God.

8

Mystery, Befuddlement, and Hospitality

The Hospitable Poem

I AM NOT WONT to quote memes (people who are wont to say "wont" usually don't cite Facebook as a source), but a while back several of my "friends" posted the following, or some variation thereof: "The fact that no one understands you doesn't make you a poet." While these posts seemed a little passive aggressive at the time, the point is well taken. Mere befuddlement does not a poem make.

There is a crucial distinction between mystery and mere befuddlement. All great poetry invites us into mystery, to some degree. As I have argued throughout this book, good poetry gestures simultaneously toward the richness of creation and toward the reality of transcendence. It is inherently anti-secular. A great poem points through the physical world toward the ineffable. In his *Letters to a Young Poet*, the great early twentieth-century poet Rainer Maria Rilke explains to the would-be artist that anyone who wishes to make art must "have courage for the most strange, the most singular and the most inexplicable that we may encounter. That mankind has in this sense been cowardly has done life endless harm; the experiences that are called 'visions,' the whole so-called 'spirit-world,' death, all those things that are so closely akin to us, have by daily parrying been so crowded out of life that the senses with which we could have grasped them are atrophied. To say nothing of God."¹ What he is describing is something like the "disenchantment" of the world, chronicled by Charles Taylor and others, which we discussed in the previous chapter. Poetry, in Rilke's conception, contributes to what has been called the "re-enchantment" of the world. Poetry gives us back mystery. It puts us in the frame of mind in which we may believe. When a poet cultivates mystery, we readers feel as if there is something that we don't quite know, and we are not only okay with not knowing but are, in fact, in some sense encouraged or inspired by the limits of our knowledge. We are delighted to know that there is more to know than what we know. We are enchanted by the possibility of transcendence.

When a poet achieves only befuddlement, on the other hand, we are left feeling as if there is something we really ought to know in order to "get" the poem but which we are simply missing. Like mystery, befuddlement may point us toward our own limitations, but not in a way that re-enchants the world. When befuddled, we are not pointed toward a mystery larger than ourselves. Rather, befuddlement just makes us feel frustrated and even angry. Such an experience can permanently turn a person cold toward poetry. Like Jacob and Esau, mystery and befuddlement come forth from the same womb and yet are worlds apart.

People who write about poetry sometimes class poems as either "difficult" or "accessible," but I am not sure those are the best categories for thinking about poetry. Instead of accessibility, which might suggest that the poem should be, in some way "easy," I prefer to think in terms of "hospitality." From Homer's epics to the latest issue of *Southern Living*, hospitality is a virtue honored in cultures all over the world and throughout human history, making it an excellent starting place for grounding an aesthetic understanding of the relationship between a poem and its reader. Moreover, hospitality is mentioned as one of the virtues expected of a leader in the church (1 Timothy 3:2 and Titus 1:8) and is one of the qualities Christ himself sees as defining the true Christian, as he says to the elect "I was hungry and you gave me food, I was thirsty and you gave me drink, I was a stranger and you welcomed me" (Matthew 25:35).

A writer does well to ask, therefore, if the poem invites the reader in or pushes the reader away. Does the poem seek communion, or does it seek to diminish the reader in some way? A mysterious poem may still be

---

1. Rilke, *Letters*, 51.

hospitable to the reader, inviting us into mystery rather than throwing up a wall of secret *gnosis*, hidden knowledge, to keep us out.

At the heart of the gnostic heresy is the assertion that salvation is by secret knowledge, that only the few with the right *gnosis* will be saved. The gnostics created dizzying mythologies and genealogies in order to keep the uninitiated on the outside. It is easy to feel that modern and postmodern poetry has done the same. Many readers give up on poetry entirely because they feel that they could never "understand" it, that it was perhaps even written just to frustrate them, to separate the in-group from the out. One might forgive general readers for concluding that poetry is a joke if it seems to be that the joke is always on the general reader.

Mystery Religions

Some contemporary writers inclined to literary populism and dedicated to restoring poetry to a larger audience, poet-essayists like Ted Kooser and Dana Gioia, see the befuddling, inhospitable nature of contemporary poetry as the reason for the decline in readership.[2] If, indeed, one compares many twentieth- and twenty-first-century poets to their Victorian predecessors, who enjoyed a wide readership with poems of narrative and didactic clarity, it is easy to get the impression that poetry at some point in the modern period became a mystery religion meant only for the few.

Some argue that the rise of English departments is in part to blame for this impression. The study of literature in English at the college level is a relatively new phenomenon, and we are just now beginning to see its effects. With more and more professors teaching poetry in the modern universities, the tendency throughout the twentieth century was to elevate to canonical status those poems that most need professors to explicate them. In other words, the poems that get attention in class are the poems that give the professors something to do with the fifty to seventy minutes of class time they have to devote to the poem. In turn, arguably, many poets began to write for explication. Poetry became "difficult" because a feedback loop existed that demanded it do so.

The great poet-critic Randall Jarrell, however, in his essay, "The Obscurity of the Poet," looked at the issue from the other end, imagining the poet saying to his audience, "Since you won't read me, I'll make sure you

2. See the chapter on "Writing for Others," in Kooser, *The Poetry Home Repair Manual,* and Gioia, *Can Poetry Matter?*

can't."[3] Jarrell, however, also acknowledges both that the intentional difficulty of high modernist poetry may be only a passing moment and that the degraded reading habits of the average American might render even a fairly simple poem too difficult for general consumption. Still, he is most likely right that it is a case of equal and opposite reactions: the reader rejects the "difficult" modern poet and the modern poet, in turn, increases the difficulty as a way of rejecting the average reader. The rift can quickly come to seem un-closable.

Whatever the cause, the past century has definitely seen the rise, perhaps even the rise to dominance, of a kind of poetry that intentionally resists its reader, that makes its own difficulty part of its subject matter. Of course, one can easily name important poets from the early twentieth century to today who have written clear, accessible, plain-spoken work: Robert Frost, James Wright, Jane Kenyon, B. H. Fairchild, to name just a few of my favorites. One can also name poets writing well before Ezra Pound whose work one might call "difficult" or even, at times, nearly incomprehensible: Edmund Spenser and John Milton, for instance. Emily Dickinson and Gerard Manley Hopkins, of course, were both writing obscure and craggy poems in the nineteenth century, though it was perhaps the modernists' love for difficulty that helped make their posthumous reputations. Still, with exceptions noted, as well as precedents, it is, on the whole, fair to say there has been a tendency in modern and postmodern verse towards a greater obscurity of meaning.

Some modern and postmodern poets have argued that difficulty is the only appropriate way to address life in the contemporary world. T. S. Eliot, whose dense and allusion-filled work has puzzled many a senior English student, asserted that "poets in our civilization, as it exists at present, must be *difficult*. Our civilization comprehends great variety and complexity, and this variety and complexity, playing upon a refined sensibility, must produce various and complex results. The poet must become more and more comprehensive, more allusive, more indirect, in order to force, to dislocate if necessary, language into his meaning."[4] By the second half of the twentieth century there was no more influential voice in English-language literature than that of Eliot, and his idea that a difficult world demands a difficult poetry came to have a powerful influence over the way poetry is written and over how it is taught in our schools and colleges.

---

3. Jarrell, *Poetry and the Age*, 12.
4. Eliot, "The Metaphysical Poets," in *Selected Essays*, 248.

Mystery, Befuddlement, and Hospitality

The prominent English poet Geoffrey Hill also embraced this emphasis on ambiguity and on difficulty, writing grammatically dense poems thick with allusion and unlikely to explain themselves. While some poets of his generation were turning to a "confessional" directness, and achieving a good deal of popular success as a result, Hill never clearly renounced the high modernist approach to poetry typified by Eliot, Pound, and Gertrude Stein. In an interview in *The Paris Review*, Hill defends "difficult poetry," arguing that "[w]e are difficult. Human beings are difficult. We're difficult to ourselves, we're difficult to each other. And we are mysteries to ourselves, we are mysteries to each other. . . . I think art has a right—not an obligation—to be difficult if it wishes. And, since people generally go on from this to talk about elitism versus democracy, I would add that genuinely difficult art is truly democratic."[5] Hill asserts that a poem that makes interpretation difficult exhibits more confidence in the reader's ability to puzzle it out, so a thorny poem is more democratic in the sense that it puts a lot of faith in the intelligence of the average reader. Hill's appeal to democracy clearly runs counter to Eliot's notable elitism, even while Hill shores up Eliot's poetics. In this way, Hill is interestingly part of a migration of "difficulty" from the high cultural conservatism of Eliot on the right to the postmodern left, a shift accelerated by the influence of European literary theory and seen in America with the association of leftist and even radical politics with the highly experimental and "difficult" group of writers known as the L=A=N=G=U=A=G=E poets, for instance.

The L=A=N=G=U=A=G=E poets (often referred to in aggregate as "langpo") began in the late seventies as a loose group of associates, including Ron Silliman, Lyn Hejinian, and Charles Bernstein, determined to create poetry that radically rejects traditional ideas about speaker and narrative. They aimed to divorce utterance from intention. Their motives were expressly political: by emphasizing language rather than meaning, they hoped to free readers to construct meaning for themselves, thus striking a blow against all forms of hegemony by refusing to impose so much as a pretense of meaning on the reader. Taking their name from the small magazine they produced and published in, *L=A=N=G-U=A=G=E*, they considered themselves to be the heirs of the American avant-garde as it developed from Louis Zukofsky to John Ashbery.

Such avant-garde poetry is characterized by a resistance to narrative, the assault on logic, the abandonment of meaning and closure, and often

---

5. Phillips, "Geoffrey Hill."

jumpy and seemingly random typography. This kind of poetry wants to jettison notions of individual voice and genius that its practitioners consider not only hopelessly romantic but also implicated in unjust economic and social structures. Bernstein's poem "Asylum," for example, is a collage assembled from a book with the Foucauldian sounding subtitle *Essays on the Social Situation of Mental Patients and Other Inmates* and his poem "Lift Off" is transcribed entirely from the correction tape of an IBM typewriter.

Whatever the poet's theory of composition, when readers encounter a line of poetry like "HH/ ie,s obVrsxr;atjrn dugh seineopcv I iibalfmgmMw" from "Lift Off," it is easy for them to feel intentionally pushed out of the poem.[6] Bernstein, in a book amusingly entitled *Attack of the Difficult Poems* evokes the same political reasoning as Hill, arguing that "'Accessibility' has become a kind of Moral Imperative based on the condescending notion that readers are intellectually challenged, and mustn't be presented with anything but Safe Poetry."[7] Hill, Bernstein, and many other contemporary poets see it as their duty to write poems that present themselves as either impenetrable to interpretation or as so fluid as to invite any interpretation the reader might desire. They thus take their stand on the side of "difficult-ly" as opposed to the "accessibility" championed by poets like Ted Kooser.

This long debate gives the impression that a poem must be either incomprehensible to the general reader or written at the second-grade reading level. Our general experience of great poems, however, tells us that this is not the case. There are great poems I fell in love with in middle school that still reward me with new depths of insight and mystery when I read them today. If we recast the question from a choice between "difficulty" and "accessibility" to a matter of reconciling hospitality and mystery, we arrive at a poetics that is more consonant with Christian orthodoxy and more agreeable to most readers without sacrificing the true depiction of our rich and multi-layered reality.

The Fine Line

A poet who wishes to walk the fine line between mystery and befuddlement must do so, to a great extent, through trial and error. If there were a simple process for producing mystery in a poem, it wouldn't be mystery. A poet must aim for mystery and revise when the poem slips into mere

---

6. Bernstein, "Lift Off," in *All the Whiskey in Heaven*, 36.
7. Bernstein, *Attack of the Difficult Poems*, 28.

befuddlement. It helps, however, to look at the work of a single poet who can illustrate both sides of the line, and perhaps no other poet has generated so much mystery and so much pure befuddlement as John Berryman in his magnum opus, *The Dream Songs*.

The poems in *The Dream Songs* are fragmentary records of the poet's trauma, particularly his father's suicide but also his own failed marriages and struggles with his destructive impulses. Berryman uses at least two distinct voices—one "Henry," who seems a stand in for the poet despite Berryman's claims otherwise, and one interlocutor who refers to Henry by the ominous nickname "Mr. Bones"—but he does not always clearly indicate who is speaking, and sometimes other voices seem to leak in. The poems are full of stream-of-consciousness phrases and images as well as jumbled references to literature, history, theology, politics, and merely personal matters. It is often hard to know what to make of these poems, which, like their author, seem sometimes in touch with some deep mystery about human suffering and sometimes merely baffled by their own existence.

I urge the reader to spend some time with the first poem of *The Dream Songs*, a moving and powerful picture of the loss of innocence. There is much that is inexplicable in the magnificent opening poem, but nothing in the poem causes the reader to feel like crucial information is simply missing.[8] Although there are many gestures in the poem toward events the details of which we are unaware of, we can be fairly certain of what sort of events they are. When, for instance, the poet proclaims that "All the world like a woolen lover / once did seem on Henry's side. / Then came a departure," although one suspects these lines are referring to the suicide of Berryman's father, one does not need this biographical information to appreciate the poem and be moved by it. We recognize it simply as another version of *Paradise Lost* or Wordsworth's lament for a lost childhood. The loss of Eden, whether personal or universal, is not a topic most readers must work hard to recognize and connect to. Similarly, when, later in the poem, he tells us that "Once in a sycamore I was glad / all at the top, and I sang[,]" we don't need to know the exact memory the poet is referencing, which Berryman's various biographers connect to several different points in his life. The powerful suggestion of Edenic innocence and its loss is particularized through the specificity of the image and yet left powerfully mysterious in its rich ambiguity. There is much we don't know, especially without making recourse to biographical studies, in this poem, but at no

---

8. Berryman, *Dream Songs*, 3.

point do we feel we need to know anything else for the poem to hit home. The universal experience of a lost happiness resonates with any human soul, and Berryman's evocative images raise the experience to the level of mystery, a mystery among the oldest of inquiries: why must we suffer, and why do we find suffering and beauty in such close proximity?

Contrastingly, Berryman's eightieth Dream Song befuddles the reader from the start. While the first poem creates mystery with a powerful image lacking a clear referent, number eighty creates mere confusion by beginning with a referentless pronoun: "It's buried at a distance, on my insistence, buried."[9] We are told that the "it" is missed by the speaker, but we are never told what (or who?) "it" is. Perhaps "it" refers to the poet's father, but perhaps not. In the next stanza, we are introduced to "The great Uh," which seems to be God himself, but it is unclear what the poet means by naming God "Uh." Throughout the Dream Songs, Berryman uses a stylized African American dialect derived from the racist minstrel shows that once toured the country. Is "Uh" more of Berryman's ubiquitous minstrel-talk, the "great Uh" meaning the "great One"? Or is it merely inarticulateness? Forced to choose between alternative readings, we are now attempting to solve the poem rather than experiencing it as art. My point is not that poems cannot be allowed to tease us *into* thought as well as out of it, only that our contemplation of, or in response to, a work of art ought to be different from our contemplation of a riddle. By the time, however, Berryman refers to a "house-guest" later in the poem, we have left off experiencing the poem and are only trying to decipher it. We start to wish we could order a decoder ring, like those offered on the old radio shows. When the frequently intrusive interlocutor of the poems finally says, "Mr Bones, what's all about?" we are likely to second the plea for clarity, for we have been given perplexity in the place of wonder.

I am not suggesting that a poem should never require knowledge beyond its own confines on the page. It is fine for a poem to require a little research or the use of good footnotes. Such a poem, however, ought to give the reader some sense of *what* to research. It ought not be inhospitable, as if carrying on a conversation from which the reader is intentionally excluded, not if it aims to be meaningful and resonant art. Gnostic exclusion is a poor aesthetic strategy. Often, it is a lazy substitution for real mystery.

Mystery relies on precision of imagery to carry the reader when the surface meaning of the poem gives out. Good ambiguity of this kind creates

---

9. Berryman, *Dream Songs*, 95.

Mystery, Befuddlement, and Hospitality

a mood and a sense of something bigger than ourselves, a powerful emotional experience even in the absence of a clear narrative. The late American experimental poet John Ashbery, in his best work, is a master of this kind of ambiguity. Consider these lines from his poem "Farm III": "Small waves strike / The dark stones. The wife reads / The letter. There is nothing irreversible[.]"[10] We don't know who "The wife" is or what is or is not irreversible, but the lines are mysteriously sad. They evoke what seems to be a desperate clinging to hope. There is not one, but rather a multitude, of implied narratives here, and the poem does not require us to choose from among them, does not set us to the task of merely deciphering the poem. In fact, one might argue that when poetry conveys such strong feeling without the use of narrative, it comes closest to being like music. To say so, of course, does not diminish the value of narrative in other poetic modes.

Having examined the strength and pitfalls of ambiguity in generating a sense of mystery, we can see that the problem with much "experimental" poetry today is not that it is too "difficult," despite its reputation as such, but rather that it is surprisingly too explicable, lacking in the mystery that can only come from the play of meaning. When one "writes" a poem by erasing every third word of another text or by recording every fiftieth entry from a dictionary, or by transcribing one's correction ribbon, one effectively removes mystery from art. This kind of anti-art is practically inevitable from a modern, secularized, dis-enchanted worldview. We shouldn't wonder that so many L=A=N=G=U=A=G=E poets produce poems of this nature, given the Marxist materialist frame through which they tend to view the world.

When procedure takes the place of meaning, a poem is drained of the possibility of wonder. Of course, even conceptual or "procedural" work can accidentally ignite a spark of mystery. When, for instance, the notorious "procedural poet" Kenneth Goldsmith transcribes hundreds of hours of traffic reports from New York radio for his book *Traffic*, some intriguingly strange language is bound to emerge, oddly enchanting lines like "Not too bad along the Tappan Zee and alternate side suspended throughout the holiday."[11] Few people, however, would desire to read the thing in its entirety, wading through endless amounts of lines like "Well, the traffic that

---

10. Ashbery, "Farm III," in *Self-Portrait*, 30.
11. Goldsmith, *Traffic*, 32.

we've been dealing with is, uh, mainly surrounding the, uh, bridges and tunnels."[12] Such work is, as the author himself has admitted, dull.[13]

Yet many of the techniques of postmodern, experimental, or avant-garde poetry are quite consonant with the Christian sense of mystery. Poet and critic Stephen Burt has pointed out a mode of contemporary poetry he terms "elliptical."[14] Elliptical poets avoid clear narratives and untroubled anecdote, "swerving away from a never-quite-unfolded backstory; they are easier to process in parts than in wholes."[15] These poets are certainly influenced by postmodern concepts of the slipperiness of language and the fluidity of identity, but their refusal to too neatly nail down meaning in a poem, their preference for indirect suggestion over direct assertion, is also quite consonant with the Christian sense of mystery. They are often saved from the tedious materiality of pure experimental poetry by a continuing commitment to lyricism, or even to beauty. Indeed several prominent poets engaged with the subject of faith, such as Scott Cairns and Mary Szybist, use techniques that could be described as "elliptical" to create poems of subtle beauty and great mystery.[16]

Regardless of the technique, we need mystery in a poem. As the contemporary poet Dean Young has said, "Some things, like sewer pipes, we want to go only in one direction. But art that is at odds with itself, its own being, that contains seeds, signs, slashes of its own demise, embodies the conflicts of what it is to be alive."[17] Life is mysterious, richer than any poem can capture, enchanted. Any reading of Holy Scripture should encourage us to see that God's creation and our existence in it are full of mystery.

Poems should reflect that experience, but they should do so without being inhospitable to the reader. This balance between mystery and hospitality, the trick of staying clear of mere befuddlement, can be difficult to achieve. It is, however, very worthwhile.

12. Goldsmith, *Traffic*, 44.
13. Perloff, *Unoriginal Genius*, 147.
14. Burt, *Close Calls*.
15. Burt, *Close Calls*, 346.
16. See Szybist's award-winning *Incarnadine* and Cairns's *Slow Pilgrim*.
17. Young, *Art of Recklessness*, 52.

Conclusion

I SOMETIMES ASK STUDENTS in my literature classes if *Hamlet* is inherently better than, say, a Spider-Man comic. Most of them are very hesitant to assert that a work of dramatic literature recognized for the last 500 years as one of humanity's greatest literary accomplishments is in any clear sense superior to a few garish and sensational pages made to be consumed and forgotten. They, in fact, think it downright snobbish, or elitist, of me to even suggest the possibility that one kind of writing might be more worth preserving and cherishing than another. They may base this view—scandalous to their fusty professor—on their personal feelings about what they would prefer to spend the semester reading, but that feeling is itself a result of the postmodern aesthetics—or anti-aesthetics—into which they have been unknowingly initiated. Even my earnest young evangelical students, who would certainly resist the suggestion that truth and goodness are "merely cultural constructs" are completely comfortable asserting that there is no such thing as *more* or *less* beauty. Yet, if the church is to be properly attentive to beauty—honoring it as a transcendental which points us to the reality of God—then we need aesthetic standards that will help us separate real beauty from cheap knock-offs. It has been the argument of this book that these aesthetic standards are readily assessable in the rich worldview of Christian orthodoxy.

Who would deny that there is such a thing as singing off-key? We expect a musical performance, while surprising and delighting us, to correspond as part of its artistic integrity to reality, in this case the mathematical and physical reality we call *music*. We may all have developed better or worse "ears" for hearing pitch, but no one says seriously that a tune is in key or out of key *to me*. We might differ in our ability to detect it, but there is a mathematical harmony at work that makes music work.

A Poetics of Orthodoxy

Thinkers associated with what we call "the eighteenth-century enlightenment" sought to establish such objective standards for other art forms. Inspired by the scientific revolution and a general faith in human reason, they sought to uncover "natural laws" that govern artistic success as surely as the natural laws of gravity and motion described by Newton govern the operation of the physical universe, and thus the modern concept of aesthetics was born. Alexander Pope's long poem *Essay on Criticism* lays out the principles of this aesthetic quest in tidy heroic couplets:

> First follow NATURE, and your Judgment frame
> By her just Standard, which is still the same:
> *Unerring Nature* still divinely bright,
> One *clear, unchang'd* and *Universal* light,
> Life, Force and Beauty, must to all impart,
> At once the *Source* and *End* and *Test* of *Art*.
> . . .
> Those RULES, of old *discover'd*, not *devis'd*,
> Are *Nature* still, but *Nature Methodiz'd*;
> *Nature*, like *Liberty*, is but restrained
> By the same Laws which first *herself* ordain'd.[1]

Pope and his fellow enlightenment faithful were confident that the "test of art" was objective, scientific principle, discernable through study and experiment. The rules of art were as preexistent and as discoverable as the laws of motion.

I think it is fair to say that this enlightenment project did not pan out. Aesthetic success proved to be more slippery than Pope supposed, and the modern age saw not an objective consensus regarding aesthetics but rather a rapid multiplication of aesthetic theories and practices followed by the widespread postmodern abandonment of the very idea of aesthetic principles and judgment. With so many different ideas of the beautiful to choose from, the Western world seems to have avoided the necessity of picking one by opting to abandon the idea of beauty all together.

But the lack of scientific standards by which to judge aesthetic efforts need not imply that aesthetic judgment is impossible. There are more things in heaven and earth than science can discern. As I hope to have shown in this book, aesthetic value can be determined in relation to another, older

---

1. Pope, *Essay on Criticism*, in *Poems of Pope*, 246–47 and 249.

CONCLUSION

effort to establish an objective understanding that corresponds to reality: Christian orthodoxy.

Contrary to widespread misunderstanding, Christian orthodoxy is not an assertion of randomly—or even strategically—chosen subjective opinions or wishes but rather a strong consensus arrived at through logical processes of inquiry and debate. In the first centuries after the incarnation of Christ and the writing of Scripture, the church put all its intellectual resources into determining the meaning of the revelation. Contrary to popular opinion in our time, they were not merely asserting their power and authority by drawing arbitrary lines around the faith. Rather, they were using a process much like our academic concept of "peer review" to sort through which opinions are reasonable understandings of the faith grounded in the teaching of Christ and his apostles and which are deviations from the message as it was first given in revelation and preserved by the first Christians.

Though not in the same sense empirical, this is a process surprisingly like modern science. Unlike modern science, however, orthodoxy is an enterprise open to conversation about meaning. In fact it is actually centered on such conversation. This cohabitation of the objective search for truth with openness to questions of purpose and meaning in human life makes Christian orthodoxy the best foundation on which to build our aesthetic judgments.

I hope this book has given the reader some sense not just of what makes a good poem good but also of why we should care. Aesthetic success is not just in the eye of the beholder. Good poems call from us the implicit or explicit acknowledgment of what, in somewhat old-fashioned terms, we can call the human condition. This condition, however, is not of our own making. Our reality has been shaped by our creator and redeemer, and, in seeking to know him, we find also a solid foundation for our creative work. In the words of Matthew 6:33, "seek first the kingdom of God and his righteousness, and all these things will be added to you."

Bibliography

Alter, Alexandra. "Web Poets' Society: New Breed Succeeds in Taking Verse Viral." *New York Times*, November 8, 2015. https://www.nytimes.com/2015/11/08/business/media/web-poets-society-new-breed-succeeds-in-taking-verse-viral.html.
Aristotle. *The Rhetoric and the Poetics of Aristotle*. Translated by Rhys Roberts and Ingram Bywater. New York: The Modern Library, 1954.
Ashbery, John. *Self-Portrait in a Convex Mirror*. New York: Penguin, 2009.
Augustine. *Confessions*. Translated by Henry Chadwick. Oxford: Oxford University Press, 1992.
Baer, William. *Writing Metrical Poetry: Contemporary Lessons for Mastering Traditional Forms*. Cincinnati: Writers Digest, 2006.
Bernstein, Charles. *All the Whiskey in Heaven*. New York: Farrar, Straus & Giroux, 2010.
———. *Attack of the Difficult Poems*. Chicago: University of Chicago Press, 2011.
Berry, Wendell. *The Country of Marriage*. San Diego: Harcourt, Brace, Jovanovich, 1975.
Berryman, John. *The Dreams Songs*. New York: Farrar, Straus and Giroux, 2007.
Beum, Robert, and Karl Shapiro. *The Prosody Handbook: A Guide to Poetic Form*. Mineola, NY: Dover, 1965.
Brenneman, Todd M. *Homespun Gospel: The Triumph of Sentimentality in Contemporary American Evangelicalism*. Oxford: Oxford University Press, 2013.
Brown, Harold O. J. *Heresies: The Image of Christ in the Mirror of Heresy and Orthodoxy from the Apostles to the Present*. Grand Rapids: Baker, 1984.
Brown, Nathan, ed. *Oklahoma Poems and their Poets*. Norman, OK: Mezcalita, 2014.
Burt, Stephen. *Close Calls with Nonsense: Reading New Poetry*. St. Paul, MN: Graywolf, 2009.
Cairns, Scott. *Slow Pilgrim: The Collected Poems*. Brewster, MA: Paraclete, 2015.
Caldecott, Stratford. *Beauty for Truth's Sake: On the Re-enchantment of Education*. Grand Rapids: Brazos, 2009.
Cannata, Raymond F., and Joshua D. Reitano. *Rooted: The Apostles Creed*. San Francisco: Doulos, 2013.
Citino, David, ed. *The Eye of the Poet*. Oxford: Oxford University Press, 2002.
Corn, Alfred. *The Poem's Heartbeat: A Manual of Prosody*. Port Townsend, WA: Copper Canyon, 2008.
Cosper, Mike. *Recapturing the Wonder: Transcendent Faith in a Disenchanted World*. Downers Grove, IL: InterVarsity, 2017.
Cropp, Jenny Yang. *String Theory*. Norman, OK: Mongrel Empire, 2015.

Bibliography

Dante. *The Divine Comedy.* Translated by Henry Wadsworth Longfellow. http://www.gutenberg.org/cache/epub/1004/pg1004-images.html.

Donne, John. *John Donne's Poetry: A Norton Critical Edition.* Edited by Donald Dickson. New York: W. W. Norton, 2007.

Doty, Mark. *The Art of Description: World into Word.* Minneapolis: Graywolf, 2010.

Douthat, Ross. *Bad Religion: How We Became a Nation of Heretics.* New York: Free, 2012.

Eco, Umberto. *Art and Beauty in the Middle Ages.* Translated by Hugh Bredin. New Haven, CT: Yale University Press, 1986.

Eliot, T. S. *The Poems of T. S. Eliot.* Edited by Christopher Ricks and Jim McCue. Baltimore: Johns Hopkins University Press, 2015.

———. *On Poetry and Poets.* New York: Noonday, 1964.

———. *Selected Essays.* New York: Harcourt, Brace and Company, 1932.

Fairchild, B. H. *The Blue Buick: New and Selected Poems.* New York: W. W. Norton, 2014.

Finch, Annie. *A Poet's Craft: A Comprehensive Guide to Making and Sharing Your Poetry.* Ann Arbor, MI: University of Michigan Press, 2012.

Frost, Robert. *The Collected Prose of Robert Frost.* Edited by Mark Richardson. Cambridge, MA: The Belknap Press of Harvard University Press, 2007.

———. *The Poetry of Robert Frost.* New York: Henry Holt, 1979.

Fujimura, Makoto. *Culture Care: Reconnecting with Beauty for our Common Life.* Downers Grove, IL: InterVarsity, 2017.

Fussell, Paul. *Poetic Form and Poetic Meter.* 2d edition. New York: McGraw-Hill, 1979.

Gioia, Dana. *Can Poetry Matter?* St. Paul, MN: Graywolf, 2002.

Gioia, Dana, David Mason, and Meg Schoerke, eds. *Twentieth-Century American Poetics: Poets on the Art of Poetry.* Boston: McGraw-Hill, 2004.

Goldsmith, Kenneth. *Traffic.* Los Angeles: Make Now, 2007.

Gwynn, R. S. *No Word of Farewell: Selected Poems, 1970–2000.* Ashland, OR: Story Line, 2000.

Hansen, Colin, ed. *Our Secular Age: Ten Years of Reading and Applying Charles Taylor.* Deerfield, IL: The Gospel Coalition, 2017.

Hardy, Edward Roche, and Cyril Richardson, eds. *Christology of the Later Fathers.* Philadelphia: Westminster, 1954.

Hart, David Bentley. *The Beauty of the Infinite.* Grand Rapids: Eerdmans, 2003.

Hayden, Robert. *The Collected Poems of Robert Hayden.* Edited by Frederick Glaysher. New York: W. W. Norton, 2013.

Herbert, George. *The Works of George Herbert.* Edited by F. E. Hutchinson. Oxford: Oxford University Press, 1941.

Hildebrand, Dietrich von. *Aesthetics.* Vol. 1. Translated by Brian McNeil. Edited by John F. Crosby. Steubenville, OH: The Hildebrand Project, 2016.

Hollander, John. *Rhyme's Reason: A Guide to English Verse.* New Haven, CT: Yale University Press, 2001.

Hopkins, Gerard Manley. *A Critical Edition of the Major Works.* Edited by Catherine Phillips. Oxford: Oxford University Press, 1986).

Houseman, A. E. *The Collected Poems of A. E. Houseman.* New York: Henry Holt, 1965.

Hudgins, Andrew. *American Rendering: New and Selected Poems.* Boston: Houghton Mifflin Harcourt, 2010.

Hughes, Langston. *Selected Poems of Langston Hughes.* New York: Vintage Classics, 1990.

Hulme, T. E. *Selected Writings.* Edited by Patrick McGuiness. New York: Routledge, 2003.

Jarman, Mark. *Unholy Sonnets.* Ashland, OR: Story Line, 2000.

Bibliography

Jarman, Mark, and David Mason, eds. *Rebel Angels: Twenty-Five Poets of the New Formalism*. Brownsville, OR: Story Line, 1996.

Jarrell, Randall. *Poetry and the Age*. New York: Vintage, 1953.

Joseph, Janine. *Driving without a License*. Farmington, ME: Alice James, 2016.

Kenner, Hugh. *The Pound Era*. Berkeley, CA: University of California Press, 1971.

Kooser, Ted. *The Poetry Home Repair Manual: Practical Advice for Beginning Poets*. Lincoln, NE: University of Nebraska Press, 2005.

Lewis. C. S. *The Complete C. S. Lewis Signature Classics*. San Francisco: Harper Collins, 2002.

———. *The Voyage of the Dawn Treader* in *The Chronicles of Narnia*. New York: Barnes and Noble, 2009.

Longenbach, James. *The Art of the Poetic Line*. Minneapolis: Graywolf, 2008.

Longfellow, Henry Wadsworth. *The Poems of Henry Wadsworth Longfellow*. Edited by Louis Untermeyer. New York: Heritage, 1943.

Lloyd, Andrew. "I Faked my Way as an Instagram Poet, and it Went Bizarrely Well." *Vice*, September 13, 2019. https://www.vice.com/en_in/article/zmjmj3/instagram-poetry-become-successful-scam.

Mariani, Paul. *Epitaphs for the Journey: New, Selected, and Revised Poems*. Eugene, OR: Cascade, 2012.

Milton, John. *Complete Poems and Major Prose*. Edited by Merritt Y. Hughes. Indianapolis: Hackett, 2003.

McGrath, Alister. *Heresy: A History of Defending the Truth*. New York: Harper One, 2009.

McPhillips, Robert. *The New Formalism: A Critical Introduction*. Cincinnati: Textos, 2005.

Nims, John Frederick, and David Mason. *The Western Wind: An Introduction to Poetry*. 4th ed. Boston: McGraw-Hill, 2000.

O'Connor, Flannery. *Mystery and Manners: Occasional Prose*. Edited by Sally and Robert Fitzgerald. New York: Farrar, Straus and Giroux, 1970.

Orwell, George. *The Orwell Reader*. New York: Harcourt, Brace and Company, 1956.

Percy, Walker. *The Message in the Bottle: How Queer Man is. How Queer Language is. And What One has to do with the Other*. New York: Picador, 1954.

Perloff, Marjorie. *Unoriginal Genius: Poetry by Other Means in the New Century*. Chicago: University of Chicago Press, 2010.

Phillips, Carl. "Geoffrey Hill, The Art of Poetry No. 80." *The Paris Review* 154 (2000). https://www.theparisreview.org/interviews/730/geoffrey-hill-the-art-of-poetry-no-80-geoffrey-hill.

Poch, John. *Dolls*. Washington, DC: Orchises, 2009.

Pope, Alexander. *Poems of Alexander Pope: Pastoral Poetry and An Essay on Criticism*. Edited by E. Audra and Aubrey Williams. London: Methuen, 1961.

Pound, Ezra. *Literary Essays of Ezra Pound*. Edited by T. S. Eliot. New York: New Directions, 1918.

———. *Selected Poems of Ezra Pound*. New York: New Directions, 1957.

Puttenham, George. *The Arte of English Poesie* (1589). In *Elizabethan Critical Essays*, vol. 2, edited by G. Gregory Smith, 1–193. London: Oxford University Press, 1904.

Ricoeur, Paul. *The Rule of Metaphor: Multi-Disciplinary Studies of the Creation of Meaning in Language*. Translated by Robert Czerny. Toronto: University of Toronto Press, 1977.

Rilke, Rainer Maria. *Letters to a Young Poet*. Translated by M. D. Herter Norton. New York: W. W. Norton, 1954.

Bibliography

Rosko, Emily, and Anton Vander Zee, eds. *A Broken Thing: Poets on the Line*. Iowa City, IA: University of Iowa Press, 2011.

Runyan, Tania. *A Thousand Vessels*. Seattle: WordFarm, 2011.

Sammon, Brendan Thomas. *Called to Attraction: An Introduction to the Theology of Beauty*. Eugene, OR: Cascade, 2017.

Schaeffer, Francis. *Art and the Bible*. Downers Grove, IL: InterVarsity, 2006.

Shakespeare, William. *The Riverside Shakespeare*. Edited by G. Blakemore Evans. Dallas: Houghton Mifflin, 1974.

Sidney, Philip. *A Critical Edition of the Major Works*. Edited by Katherine Duncan-Jones. Oxford: Oxford University Press, 1989.

Smith, G. Gregory, ed. *Elizabethan Critical Essays*. Oxford: Oxford University Press, 1904.

Smith, James K. A. *Desiring the Kingdom: Worship, Worldview, and Cultural Formation*. Grand Rapids: Baker Academic, 2009.

———. *How (Not) to be Secular: Reading Charles Taylor*. Grand Rapids: Eerdmans, 2014.

———. *You are What You Love: The Spiritual Power of Habit*. Grand Rapids: Brazos, 2016.

Swenson, Karen. *A Pilgrim into Silence*. Rochester, NY: Tiger Bark, 2008.

Szybist, Mary. *Incarnadine*. St. Paul, MN: Graywolf, 2013.

Taylor, Charles. *A Secular Age*. Cambridge, MA: The Belknap Press of Harvard University Press, 2007.

Walker, Jeanne Murray. *New Tracks, Night Falling*. Grand Rapids: Eerdmans, 2009.

Weil, Joe. *The Great Grandmother Light: New and Selected Poems*. New York: New York Quarterly, 2013.

Whitman, Walt. *Leaves of Grass*. Edited by Michael Moon. New York: W. W. Norton, 2002.

Whittier, John Greenleaf. *The Poems of John Greenleaf Whittier*. Edited by Louis Untermeyer. New York: Heritage, 1945.

Wilbur, Richard. *Collected Poems: 1943–2004*. Orlando: Harcourt, 2004.

Williams, William Carlos. *I Wanted to Write a Poem: The Autobiography of the Works of a Poet*. New York: New Directions, 1958.

———. *Paterson*. New York: New Directions, 1963.

———. *Selected Poems*. Edited by Charles Tomlinson. New York: New Directions, 1985.

Wilson, James Matthew. *The Vision of the Soul: Truth, Goodness, and Beauty in the Western Tradition*. Washington, DC: The Catholic University of America Press, 2017.

Wiman, Christian. *Every Riven Thing*. New York: Farrar, Straus and Giroux, 2010.

Wordsworth, William. *The Lyrical Ballads: 1798–1805*. London: Methuen, 1959.

Wright, Franz. *Walking to Martha's Vineyard*. New York: Alfred A. Knopf, 2008.

Wyatt, Thomas. *The Poems of Sir Thomas Wiat*. Vol. 1. Edited by A. K. Foxwell. New York: Russell & Russell, 1964.

Yeats, William Butler. *The Collected Works of W. B. Yeats*. Vol. 1. Edited by Richard J. Finneran. New York: Macmillan, 1983.

Young, Dean. *The Art of Recklessness: Poetry as Assertive Force and Contradiction*. Minneapolis: Greywolf, 2010.

Subject Index

Allegory, 91–93
Aristotle, 99, 104, 105
Ascetism, 11
Atheism, 66
Amateurism, 3–4
Apostles' Creed, 5, 11–12
Aquinas, Thomas, see Thomas Aquinas
Ashbery, John, 29–30, 111, 115
Auden, W.H., 54–55, 77
Augustine, Saint, 9, 13, 14–15, 42, 53–54, 65–67, 69, 73
Avant-garde, 111–12, 116

Bach, Johann Sebastian, 49, 73
Being, 67, 71–72
Bernstein, Charles, 39, 111, 112
Berry, Wendell, 15
Berryman, John, 77, 113–14
Bishop, Elizabeth, 77, 85
Blake, William, 7, 14, 87
Blank verse, 86
Blasphemy, 57
Bonhoeffer, Dietrich, 62
Book of Common Prayer, 11
Brenneman, Todd, 45
Brown, Harold O.J., 9, 14
Brown, Margaret Wise, 33
Buckley, William F., 105
Burnand, Eugene, 17
Bunyan, John, 93
Burt, Stephen, 116

Caldecott, Stratford, 78–79

Cairns, Scott, 116
Carvaggio, Michelangelo Merisi da, 17, 47
Coleridge, Samuel Taylor, 95
Collins, Billy, 97
Common grace, 2
Communion, 21–22, 24, 96–97
Cosper, Mike, 93
Couplets, 85–86
Consonants, 35
Creeley, Robert, 88
Cropp, Jenny Yang, 23–24
Cross and crucifixion, 46–48

Dante Alighieri, 13, 45, 57, 78, 92, 93, 97, 104
Dickinson, Emily, 5, 110
Dickerson, Matthew, 8
Docetism, 10
Donne, John, 39, 81–82
Dostoevsky, Fyodor, 46, 49
Doty, Mark, 32–33

Ecce Homo, 47
Eco, Umberto, 12, 91, 97
Elitism, 48–49, 117
Eliot, T.S., 7, 22, 23, 38, 40, 45, 77, 86, 102–3, 110, 111
Enlightenment, the, 118

Fairchild, B.H., 61, 62, 73–74, 87, 110
Finch, Annie, 23, 77
Formalist, The, 77
Free verse, 77, 86–88

Subject Index

Frost, Robert, 35, 44–45, 72, 77, 79, 84–85, 86, 89, 98, 110
Fujimura, Makoto, 7

Ginsberg, Allen, 88, 101–2
Gioia, Dana, 77, 109
Gnosticism, 1, 8–15, 19–20, 21, 41, 43, 54, 66, 91–92, 97, 109
Goldsmith, Kenneth, 115–16
Gregory of Nazianzus, 21
Gregory of Nyssa, 68, 70
Gregson, Tyler Knott, 42–43
Gywnn, R.S., 83–84

Haiku, 18, 22, 88
Hart, David Bentley, 64, 67–69, 73
Hayden, Robert, 50
Hecht, Anthony, 77
Hejinian, Lyn, 111
Herbert, George, 36, 45
Hesiod, 52
Hildebrand, Dietrich von, 63–64, 72–73
Hill, Geoffrey, 111, 112
Homer, 21, 22, 39, 43, 98, 104
Hopkins, Gerard Manley, 7, 39–40, 50–51, 62, 71, 74, 102, 110
Hospitality, 108–109, 112
Houseman, A.E., 55–56
Howard, Henry, 81, 86
Hudgins, Andrew, 77, 99
Hughes, Langston, 43–44
Hulme, T.E., 76–77

Iambic pentameter, 87
Imago Dei, 57, 59
Incarnation, 21, 64, 71
Iconoclasm, 17
Imagism, 18, 25
Iraneus, 9
Instagram, 42–43

Jarman, Mark, 45, 77, 84
Jarrell, Randall, 109–10
Joseph, Janine, 32
Justice, Donald, 77

Kapur, Rupi, 42
Kenner, Hugh, 18
Kenyon, Jane, 23, 110
Kincade, Thomas, 41
Kinnell, Galway, 32
KJV, 87
Kooser, Ted, 50, 109, 112

L=A=N=G=U=A=G=E, 39, 111, 115
Levertov, Denise, 45, 86
Lewis, C.S., 62, 72, 73, 90
Liturgy, 1, 20
Logical positivism, 38–39, 102
Logos, 78, 84, 94
Longfellow, William Wadsworth, 4, 103–4
Lowell, Robert, 77

Mariani, Paul, 22–23, 45–46
Maritain, Jacques, 67
McGrath, Alister, 9
Measure, 77
Meter, 35
Milton, John, 7, 14, 34, 53, 86, 93, 110, 113
Music, 24–25, 117

Newton, Isaac, 92, 93, 118
Nine Inch Nails, 73
Norman conquest, 28–29, 56–57, 76

O'Connor, Flannery, 40–41, 52–53
Orwell, George, 28–29
Ovid, 52

Painting, 24
Percy, Walker, 96
Petrarca, Francesco, 79
Plato, 10, 70, 73
Poch, John, 47–48
Pope, Alexander, 85, 118
Postmodernism, 5–6, 9, 63, 83, 92, 95–96, 110–11, 116, 117, 118
Pound, Ezra, 18–19, 28, 72, 77, 102, 103, 110, 111
Prosody, 76, 82
Protestantism, 11, 63, 81, 93

Subject Index

Puttenham, George, 104–5

Resurrection, 12, 20, 21, 46
Ricoeur, Paul, 95–96
Rilke, Rainer Maria, 61–62, 107–8
Rimbaud, Arthur, 27
Roethke, Theodore, 72
Runyan, Tania, 98

Sacraments, 95–96
Sammon, Brendan Thomas, 67, 71
Sestinas, 85
Schaeffer, Francis, 59, 63
Shakespeare, William, 22, 41, 54, 75, 81, 86, 94, 117
Shelly, Percy, 7
Sidney, Sir Philip, 52
Silliman, Ron, 111
Smith, James K.A., 15, 69
Snyder, Gary, 88
Sonnets, 79–84
Spenser, Edmund, 93, 97, 110
Stallings, A.E., 77
Stevens, Wallace, 22
Stein, Gertrude, 111
Stewardship, 7
Swenson, Karen, 86–87
Szybist, Mary, 116

Taylor, Charles, 11, 14, 92, 93, 94, 96, 108
Tennyson, Alfred Lord, 75
Thomas Aquinas, 71
Thomas, Dylan, 85
Thomas, R.S., 45

Tolkien, J.R.R., 8
Tradition, 39–40
Transcendentals (truth, goodness, and beauty), 4–5, 65, 69, 73, 117

Universities, 3, 109

Villanelles, 85
Virgil, 31–32, 39, 104
Vowels, 33–34

Wabi-sabi, 56
Walker, Jeanne Murray, 100–101
Wallace, Ron, 32
Weil, Joe, 98
Western Wind, The, 33–34, 35
Whitman, Walt, 75, 87–88
Whittier, John Greenleaf, 46–48, 75
Wilbur, Richard, 45, 77, 98, 99
Williams, William Carolos, 18, 25, 30–31, 77, 86, 88, 102–3
Wiman, Christian, 58–59
Wilson, James Matthew, 67, 69
Wordsworth, William, 28, 86, 113
Wright, Franz, 58
Wright, James, 110
Wyatt, Thomas, 80–81

Yeats, William Butler, 29, 35, 69–70, 72, 77
Young, Dean, 116

Zukofsky, Louis, 111

Scripture Index

OLD TESTAMENT

Genesis
1:2	77
1:31	10, 12

Psalms
1	20
18	20
19	94
23	54
27:4	4
119:68	4

NEW TESTAMENT

Matthew
6:33	119
25:35	108

John
1:1	78, 94
1:14	10, 21
10:10	69
14:6–7	4

Romans
1:20	91
8:20–23	15

1 Corinthians
10:23	58

Ephesians
4:29	56–57

Philippians
4:8	3, 5, 46, 69

Colossians
1:17	78

1 Timothy
3:2	108

Titus
1:8	108
3:9	10

Hebrews
11:13–14	41

Jude
3	7

www.ingramcontent.com/pod-product-compliance
Lightning Source LLC
Chambersburg PA
CBHW020854160426
43192CB00007B/925